MY BEING AND CALLING
A Journey in God

—❦—

CAPTAIN MOTHER
OLUFUNMILAYO HASSON

MY BEING AND CALLING
A Journey in God

CAPTAIN MOTHER
OLUFUNMILAYO HASSON

MEREO
Cirencester

Mereo Books
1A The Wool Market Dyer Street Cirencester Gloucestershire GL7 2PR
An imprint of Memoirs Publishing www.mereobooks.com

My Being and Calling: 978-1-86151-892-7

First published in Great Britain in 2018
by Mereo Books, an imprint of Memoirs Publishing

Copyright ©2018

Captain Mother Olufunmilayo Hasson has asserted her right under the Copyright Designs and Patents Act 1988 to be identified as the author of this work.

This book is a work of fiction and except in the case of historical fact any resemblance to actual persons living or dead is purely coincidental.

A CIP catalogue record for this book is available from the British Library.

This book is sold subject to the condition that it shall not by way of trade or otherwise be lent, resold, hired out or otherwise circulated without the publisher's prior consent in any form of binding or cover, other than that in which it is published and without a similar condition, including this condition being imposed on the subsequent purchaser.

The address for Memoirs Publishing Group Limited can be found at
www.memoirspublishing.com

The Memoirs Publishing Group Ltd Reg. No. 7834348

The Memoirs Publishing Group supports both The Forest Stewardship Council® (FSC®) and the PEFC® leading international forest-certification organisations. Our books carrying both the FSC label and the PEFC® and are printed on FSC®-certified paper. FSC® is the only forest-certification scheme supported by the leading environmental organisations including Greenpeace. Our paper procurement policy can be found at www.memoirspublishing.com/environment

Typeset in 12/18pt Century Schoolbook
by Wiltshire Associates Publisher Services Ltd. Printed and bound in Great Britain by Printondemand-Worldwide, Peterborough PE2 6XD

CONTENTS

	Acknowledgements	
1.	Early Days	1
2.	The Scars of Affectionate Memory	5
3.	An Unmissable Event	12
4.	What Matters Most	20
5.	Sometimes Things Just Happen	25
6.	Return to Home Base	37
7.	A New Dawn	47
8.	Casualties and Brutalities	54
9.	Appreciating Goodness in Others	62
10.	My Struggles and Manifestations	66
11.	Climbing a Slippery Ladder	72
12.	Abundant Blessings	83
13.	Eclipses and Conflicts	91
14.	Financial Boom and Doom	99
15.	Walking in a Minefield	102
16.	Beyond Belief Encounters	111
17.	Jerusalem - Israel Pilgrimages	160
18.	My Moment of Religious Joy Captain Mother Ordination	168

ACKNOWLEDGEMENTS

All thanks to the Spirit within me, shouting without a sound, who has made it possible to pour out the abundant wealth of thoughts, experience and revelations lingering within me.

Huge thanks to Hugh, my darling husband, and our kids for their understanding and for bearing with my shortcomings. Great appreciation to them for sensing and seeing goodness in all that I hauled aside, and encouraging me in writing about the voyage of my life.

I dedicate my book to all those devoted mothers who, just like my mother, have loved and lost despite giving all they have in sacrifice for their children's survival. Also, I write for fellow spiritualists with big dreams and no resources but who have the backing of God, just like me.

Chapter 1

EARLY DAYS

This book is not about my destination in life; that was set before my birth. Rather, it is about the things that happened along the way.

    I was born almost 70 years ago into a typical ethnic royal family in Ogun State, Nigeria. My father, John Mawobe (Eleyinwa of Eyinwa) was the village head cum church lay reader and my grandfather was the local church patron. From factual stories passed down, my family has always played the leadership and royal roles because of our ancestral position in the clan.

Continuity of the royal heritage is at the heart of my family. I was brought up surrounded by royal protocols. My name, Adejoko, identifies my integrity within my royal family. I cherish that; it is good to hold on to the creditability, respect and confidence it gives me.

Captain Mother Hasson flanked by her family's royal maces

The story passed down by the family has it that when my grandfather, Pa Joseph Osobanjo Osokoya, brought Christianity to our village of Eyinwa, he insisted that the practices of witchcraft and sorcery be abolished. This brought open confrontation between him and some new converts. Great antagonism arose against him amongst the congregation and threats were made against his life. But he firmly stood his ground, insisting that all Christians, both old and new converts, must put away paganism and develop the practice of Christianity outwardly and inwardly. He told them to get in get along with others, or get out of the Church. He told them to put God before all deities, because God is the Pre-Eminence. However, the opposition leader publicly boasted and swore by all his gods and deities that he had powers to end my grandfather's life, and he would accomplish his deadly mission within seven days.

My grandfather immediately called a family meeting for a briefing. He let everybody talk. Unanimously, they agreed that he should return to his ancestral home, Iloda, to report and seek for help. My great grandfather was born at Iloda, and my grandfather and father were also born there – a house through time. He did travel back to his cradle and they camped him in the ancestral inner chambers, robed and girdled, for three days for spiritual cleansing – no visitors, no food, no drink. On the third day, when he was released, every hair on his body had turned grey with age. He looked twenty years older than he was.

He was now advised by the King, Moloda of Odogbolu, to go and show himself to his opponent, the man who had vowed to kill him. On returning to the village, he went straight to his assailant to show him that he was still alive. His opponent did not recognise him. Onlookers were astonished at how fast he had aged. Now, it was my grandfather's turn to draw his straw. We fight the way we do for the delight of the things we cherish and the people we love. You cannot sleep with the enemy and call yourself free. He told his opponent to go and sleep. He did, but never woke up.

My grandfather after his ordeal did not allow his pains to deter him from following God's purpose in his life. He picked the people who were committed workers in the Church, and together they served the Community. His faith did not stop the pains and injuries which he received, but it hastened his recovery.

Chapter 2

THE SCARS OF AFFECTIONATE MEMORY

I never knew my natural mother, Bea A'kiite, as she died in my early childhood. The third of her parents' three girls, she was an Albino, petite and frail physically but reportedly beautiful to behold. It is not the size that makes a gem, it is the cut. Everybody who knew her constantly paid homage to her kind and caring heart. I inherited my fair complexion from her and probably my weakness in life, my honesty.

My parents married early in 1930 but they waited until 1936 for their first child, a son who was instantly accorded the right of leadership and reign. However, because there was a slight delay in my mother giving birth, my father took another wife. That was the pattern of matrimony then.

Not long after, in 1946, my mother gave birth to another son. He is now Professor Israel Olu Osokoya, former Head of Institute of Education, University of Ibadan. He is an educationist, a Professor of Education and author of many books. There is no competition between us, only comparison. Although we are distinctively similar, we have discovered our individual uniqueness in life.

My position as the last born and the supposed reincarnation of my ancestral paternal grandmother earned me a lot of respect and pampering in the community. Elderly women and new wives preferred calling me by my native rank 'Erelu' (women's leader) thereby according me the respect that goes with it. Right from a tender age, I have learnt not to define myself by what I do but by who I am. It was instilled in me to walk with dignity and self-esteem. However, in a small village like mine, what people think about you matters, but what you think about yourself is paramount.

There are times in our lives when nature puts us in situations we can neither see nor understand. I was raised in a polygamous family by my nurse, who eventually became my stepmother.

In 1955 there was an outbreak of influenza in my village and my family was not spared the deadly smallpox virus. Both my mother and I were sick with smallpox. It was a very severe attack which lasted for almost two years. I was covered with enough scars to last me a lifetime. We were hidden away; no contact with people except the local herbalists, Baba Otusanya (Oguntun Quarters) and Baba Awofala (Arintun Quarters) and a kola nuts trader, Abigail Alaba, who had previously been adopted as a daughter by my natural mother. Though her village was seven miles away, she would trek to see us and be with us before the cock crowed in the morning. Abigail Alaba was the kola nut seller, the adopted daughter who eventually turned herself to be our nurse. She was God sent.

Abigail was a local beauty. She was tall and gorgeous. Although an illiterate, she was witty with the use of words, similes and metaphors, and very humorous. She was very strict and some people scorned her for not bearing a child. I was raised to be humble without forgetting my communal position. My stepmother embedded in me, right from childhood, the spirit of self-esteem and confidence and determination which led me to find my path in life. She was my first teacher; she taught me facts of life even before I knew what life was all about. She was there for me when my natural mother was gone. Abigail Alaba was my heroine and champion.

The two elderly kind-spirited men, Pa Otusanya and Awofala, dug roots and plucked leaves, mixed them together and most of the time boiled and cooked them for us to drink. Every day they would blend palm kernels with honey and other ingredients to adorn both my mother and myself to cool our burning skin. The pair were brilliant, dedicated and deeply admired in the community. They embraced and practised the traditional mystic healing. To me, what they were doing was physically and mentally uplifting. They were warm and wise.

Baba Awofala was a brilliant storyteller and a leading man with character. He revived our weakened spirits with local songs and tales. His stories were of various theme; of powerful hunters on expeditions, of animals in the market and assembly days. They were warm as well as powerful; mind-blowing and thought-provoking stories and very hard to resist. The ones I found most uproariously funny were the tales of Tortoise and his wife Yarinbo.

Baba Awofala was imaginative and artistic. He would say that it is not how a man feels when he visits you that matters, but how he feels when he leaves you. He was kind and sensitive.

How I used to love the early morning visits of the two herbalists. Their daily visits gladdened my heart. They will never be forgotten, because they were extraordinary, remarkable people. They did everything humanly possible to save our lives. They treated us with skills, care and commitment.

I cannot recollect any laughter or amusement, but every evening, Baba Otusanya would fetch a keg of palm wine and sprinkle our room and the entire compound with it. He religiously did this, in his own words "to ward off evil and invite the ancestors to take care of us". The dregs of the wine were for the sick. So, every evening I was always dead drunk before going to bed! It is only in my adult life that I realised what the kind herbalist was doing. He was using palm wine to sanitise the environment and getting us drunk to aid much-needed sound sleep. Whatsoever his motive was, it worked well for me because I was hooked on palm wine!

As times went by, I could tell just by tasting the wine which area of the village it was tapped from. Also, I would correctly give the time of tapping and whether it was diluted or not. If left for a period without being served, palm wine would ferment, becoming strong to taste and highly intoxicating. Some people prefer it this way as its consumption is slow, but the effects linger on longer. Some take strong wine in order to have courage to confront their fears. An irate husband would intentionally get drunk in order to confront his in-laws about their daughter's misconduct and shortcomings, so a bit of intoxicating palm wine would help push out what was in him!

Palm trees around swamps produce light, less sugary wine. This is good for women and general daily consumption. However, upper hill or farmland palm trees produce highly concentrated wine; very sweet but intoxicating. This type of wine is always in high demand by the Elders and as such is served during burial rites (to drown the sorrows of mourners), circumcision rites (to reduce the pain of fresh, sensitive wounds) and during wedding ceremonies.

At a wedding, the groom would present a keg of palm wine to all the Elders. It is his way of saying "my gift will make room for me". He would serve it, constantly shaking the keg indicating the volume left. At the end, the groom would serve himself the last cup before leaving to meet his new wife. The last cup is always believed to hold the secret of early conception. Funny, clever and absolutely filthy. Our Elders believe that what you are carrying inside you is the answer to your promise.

During this time, the local palm wine tapper was a stranger in our community. He was a middle-aged drunkard called Alonje. Because he was always fidgeting, whispering and talking to himself, he was not accorded much respect and regarded as a nonentity, a person of no account.

I on the contrary found Alonje to be explosively funny. He was old but not mature; growing up is not for everybody. I found his stories and jokes thrilling, fresh and wonderfully engaging just like his early morning palm wine supply, an utter delight.

Chapter 3

AN UNMISSABLE EVENT

One cold thunderous December morning, Baba Awofala was late in coming to see us. Because it had rained throughout the previous night, we all thought his hut was either waterlogged or flooded. It was unusual for him to be late.

Another unusual thing was that my mother became very agitating and restless. She was almost screaming, calling out for him to hurry up, because there was something she needed to tell him. At the same time, she was checking on me to see if I was still beside her. That was strange as I did not have enough strength to sit or stand, let alone talk of running away or leaving the hut. We had all been together on the same mats for almost eight months and were bedridden. Surely, something was afoot.

My mother woke up talking loudly. Despite the chilling cold and raging thunder, she demanded to have all the doors and windows opened. There was a great silence in the hut, even with the roaring thunder. She started singing praises of championship to herself, consolation and encouragement that her journey would be easier as she was not travelling in isolation. She asked to be helped into a sitting position. Then she dragged me to her, caressing me, telling me that her plane was on standby outside and that she was ready for a journey from which she would take a long time to return. Also, she hinted that there were people on the plane who were in one accord with her, singing the same songs, with the same pulse and rhythm. She prayed for me and advised that I must not let my present situation determine my destiny.

The thunder, the falling trees, and the unstoppable torrential rainfalls were all signs of identification to the celestial plane and crew. They came for her and not me. She told me that she would make the journey for the two of us. By this journey, she was disconnecting herself and me from pains. She gave me the assurance that I would be healed and that help was on the way.

On that cold morning of 12th December, my mother called our nurse, Abigail Alaba, giving her some specific requests and instructions. Firstly, my mother asked her to marry my father. She begged her to please take good care of my father and the family. She explained to her that she had to embark on her journey, leaving me behind. My father, she explained, though a strict disciplinarian, was in fact very compassionate and with time, the nurse would understand him well. She urged her to build a future within our family.

Abigail's response was that my father would never understand or recognise her as a wife. My mother said to her that people do not care much about what you know until they know how much you care. With tearful eyes, my mother pleaded with our nurse to peel off the lesser things in order to uncover greater things. Assuring her, she told her she had been brought into our home for a purpose. Though she might regard our home as a prison now, eventually the reality would dawn on her that It was a palace.

The nurse promised to think about the requests and said she would give her answers later. "Absolutely, positively, no!" said my mother. "I do not have time. I am leaving behind what I cared for and you have been picked to take over. Realise that my position is hard, so rethink and give me a positive answer." She advised our nurse to flush away fears from her heart and take me as her child.

All the while, we were still waiting for Baba Awofala. When he eventually arrived, he had his own story to tell. As custom demands, experienced herbalists must know what and when to gather before brewing. Most of the time, it is best to pluck herbs in the early morning when the leaves are fresh and wet with dew. Timing counts also because some leaves must be plucked before sunrise and incantations need to be recited before cutting the stems and roots. Sometimes, herbalists faced dangers and challenges in the course of getting their patients healed. Endurance is the secret of life. Many a time, Baba Awofala told us that some powerful people in the community had told him to wash his hands off, looking after me in particular. He was threatened and so also were his wives. His maize farm was set ablaze by unknown people; on many occasions he was threatened with exclusion from the community elders. Sticking to his guns, he told them that failure was not an option in his life and he would finish the task. People used this to label him as an outcast. Baba Awofala was an exceptional person.

As Baba Awofala stepped inside the hut, my mother shouted at him, "The big wind has blown, the tree is bent and uprooted. Where have you been since morning? Have you seen our visitors outside? You delayed our departure."

My mother said that she was desperate and that was why she took a desperate decision; she had to do what she did in order to get the job done. She explained that the waiting plane had one seat for the journey and she had decided to go on the journey, leaving me behind. Everyone around was perplexed at her riddles.

"Erelu" she said, pointing to my skinny frame, "was born with a purpose and the potential for greatness. She has an appointment with destiny and her life will change for good. Affirmatively, Erelu will not die. When she was born, her father consulted an oracle to enquire about the child's destiny. The deity made us realise that Erelu would grow to become a great woman in the community and will eventually go abroad. She is a traveller. She will return home to develop the community. She will be a mother to the whole community; she will outlive all her enemies. Erelu is a crown child. What could not happen in her early life will be released to her at her later life and old age."

Then she implored them not to give up on me. She was right about the predictions. However, there was danger in seeking to know the secret of what the future holds, because those who know your destiny will always be your stalkers.

The old man replied that nature was against him. When he had left his hut at dawn, he had been met by a woman who had not answered his repeated greetings. Instantly, a chill had run through his spine, he said. On reaching the forest, the tree he sought would not release its leaves, despite his incantations. He peeled off the bark, but there was no juice. It was dry. It was as if the tree was barren. He felt helpless, as he could neither explain nor control the situation around him. He had returned without a single herb, disappointed and frustrated. His story made me shiver.

Towards the evening, my mother started singing and praying for everyone. She blessed and praised the medicine men for their courage and love, urging them to be strong and not to be disappointed by oncoming events. Then Baba Awofala asked her to be still and rest. She replied that she would rest where she was going. She conversed with him about expectations and acceptance. Then she became very emotional and wept bitterly. She dragged herself across the mat and sat up, resting on the bamboo and palm leaves matted wall. Dragging me on to her lap, she held me resting on her chest and prayed for me. Her tears fell on my head and rolled down my face. I could feel them; her tears were hot. My mother called me by my native name and said "You will not die until you achieve what you are created to do and be". All the Elders said "Amen" in chorus. It was heartrending. She died in the evening of that day.

So at a tender age, I lost my mother, but my love for her never dies; it was not buried in the grave. The bond between me and my mother lives on beyond death; it cannot be broken even after death.

For two years, I was kept in isolation; away from family members, relations, all and sundry. I was fed on vegetables and palm wine and adorned with medicinal oils and charms. The only people in my life were the medicine men and my nurse. They cared immensely for me.

Every day, I struggled in my mind, asking where my father and the other family members were, why we never received any visitor and why my only playmates were the two medicine men. If only I had known then what I now know. My grief was like a strong water current; it nearly sank me.

My mother's two siblings, my aunts were forbidden to see us, because they were maliciously accused of witchcraft and sorcery. Our whereabouts were kept secret from them. On my father's side, I had four uncles and an auntie, but we did not see any of them. My paternal grandmother was alive but old. She was afraid of offending her children, so she kept away.

My sickness kept me away from the village for almost three years, during which time my only contacts were my nurse and the two elderly medicine men. To me, this period of hibernation served as my early schooling. I learned more from them than anyone could imagine. I grew older than my age. My language was metaphoric and incantational. My water was palm wine and my food mainly herbs and roots. From head to toe, my nakedness was covered with mixed layers of honey, palm oil, camwood and charcoal.

Now my critics are angry because they do not know the source of my prowess. Search no further. Just go into my past with your imaginative mind!

Chapter 4

WHAT MATTERS MOST

I was not prepared for the outside world, the real world. The two medicine men, accompanied by my nurse, brought me back to my home. There were no welcoming drums or cheering crowd. I was met with mixed feelings and the entire village was nervous. Some people saw my presence as a threat, for various reasons. Some believed that my sickness was caused by the Deity and with its marks all over my body, I was untouchable. Others were afraid that smallpox was contagious and its virus could still spread like wildfire. They preferred that I be kept perpetually away from them in the forest hut. The handful who were happy to see me gave me a new name, 'Olorunju', meaning 'God is the greatest'.

My father now suddenly surfaced. My escorts were greeted pleasantly and a bottle of schnapps gin was opened and consumed, by the few elders around, to thank the Ancestors for my safe return and recovery. Moving from a familiar state into an unfamiliar position was not convenient for me.

Though I was now at home with my father, he was a stranger to me. He was brushing against me but not touching me. His discussions with my nurse were about where to keep me. His concern was more about where to keep me and not where I had been. That did hurt. I was starving for his love and companionship, but his hands were folded. Who was this stranger? I find this part of my life story very depressing, but the past cannot always be left behind. My future is akin to my past.

My caring nurse was not listened to me and my voice was not heard because I was shouting without making a sound - the sound of silence.

Still standing, frozen on a spot, my worst habit came to the fore. My temper rose within me. I called by father by his name, Mawobe. He jerked, looked at me, and burst into tears. It was an emotional release.

A mere sense of compassion and kindness helps us to hear those who have no voice.

Long after sunset, my father escorted me to our ancestral house under the cover of night and handed me over to my paternal grandmother. My grandfather lived with her there until he died in 1955. She was happy to see me. I was introduced to the entire household in the morning. The surrounding air was so thick with fury and rage it could be sliced with a knife; the atmosphere was toxic. The tension was as tight as a shopping trolley. They were my extended family, but I was a loner amongst them. All I wanted was peace, but I prepared for war. I became mute; kept to myself.

Two of her sons lived there also. The third son, Uncle Robert, was a Lagos-based tailor. He seldom came home. He was married to a black ebony lady, Arondu. They both lived far away in Lagos Mainland, Abeokuta Street, Ebute Metta. They were a very quiet couple. My Uncle Robert had a mild disability; he was a chronic stammerer. He barely conversed with anyone; his wife was his mouthpiece. She could read him like a book. They were childless.

My Uncle Isaac was the local Councillor and also a produce buyer. He was a leading man with character; tall, elegant and handsome. An absolute charmer, entirely loveable. I saw in him the excellency of dignity and power. He lived lavishly. My Uncle Isaac was the envy of everyman. He was married to Opelenge (the slimming one). She was a soft-spoken, calm and exceptionally glamorous lady. They were stinking rich but childless. Their family had a dinner timetable and every time, the presentation was superb, very classy. Food was served in Pyrex bowls with matching covers. The dinner plates and soup plates were always of the same design, everything to match. Spoons were of stainless steel. Plastic was never heard of in the household; it was an abomination to even mention the word in the living quarters. The only sight of plastic was on the cocoa farms diluting and stocking Gamiline 20 solutions for parasites.

Breakfast at 8 am was local oat and fried bean cakes. Their lunch, always served at 2 pm, was boiled rice served with freshwater fish in tomato sauce. A bottle of Heineken beer was always on the table. I grew up to recognise affluence, and the daily enjoyment of a bottle of neck foil wrapped, room temperature Heineken beer was one.

My uncle's butler would open the beer bottle and rinsed the glass tumbler with a few drops. Uncle Isaac would then have a sip in acknowledgement, nodding his head in appreciation. The bottle contents would then be slowly drained along with lunch. After lunch, my uncle would wash his hands in lavender soap water and wipe them on the white napkins presented by his butler. If he was not satisfied with the napkins, or wanted to say that they were dirty, he would wipe his hands on the butler's apron. He would then lift the beer bottle and drain whatever was left on to his hands, rubbing them together and smiling in satisfaction. This was living life to the fullest; not just existing. To crown it all, he would light a stick of his favourite cigarette, Craven A, draw a lungful and puff out the smoke for onlookers to inhale.

Evening dinner was normally pounded yam served with fresh vegetable soup, always a feast for the eyes. Bluntly speaking, my Uncle Isaac had great taste and a quality of life. Having this lifestyle in a Nigerian village in 1958 was surely a taste of heaven on earth. They were the poshest couple in the village.

My Uncle Titus was the complete opposite of his brother. He was a farmer and an illicit distiller, and he loved and respected older, mature women. He was a kind giver. Every day from his farm, he would bring home yellow yams and tubers of water yams. My grandmother was a good cook. She was an expert in preparing giddily delightful pounded yam meals; hugely enjoyable.

My two uncles were from the same parents, but their choices differed. They were created differently. To me, the choices they made revealed the nature of their characters.

Chapter 5

SOMETIMES THINGS JUST HAPPEN

My lack of preparation and classroom teaching slowed down my educational success. When all the children of my age were in primary elementary school, I was always alone at home. As luck would have it, a girl of my age lived close by and became my regular playmate. I visited her home one day and asked for drinking water. Her mother dashed across the room and chased me out of the house with curses and insults. My offence? None. She just did not want me touching her things and warned me never to drink from her pot. Some people have narrow minds and wide mouths.

I ran back home and cried myself to sleep. I must say that not everyone present supported the woman. In fact, an elderly woman condemned her totally for displaying symptoms of her family's peculiar hereditary illness - madness. Life is not fair. How do you deal with unbearable situation like this? Would I ever be happy in life?

My ordeal was reported to my grandmother by a young lady called Tinuade. After my ordeal, we became very close friends. She advised me that whenever problems arise, I should not run but stand my ground, because luck favours only the brave. When life knocks you down, do not stay down, bounce back. She taught me how to restrain my anger in order to gain conquest over my enemies. Tinuade was a real live wire to me. She was older and wiser.

Tinuade was an absolutely beautiful lady. She was a succulent person in a beautifully cast frame, fresh and ripe. Just looking at her would send a rush of blood to the head of any man. She was my kind of girl.

My father visited us one evening at the ancestral house and informed us that he was visiting Ibefun to see his second wife and children. Without giving it a thought, I demanded that he let me travel with him. That would give me the opportunity of seeing my brother. He agreed. My life was about to change.

It was three miles from our village to Ibefun and normally, it took half an hour to trek. Every market day, traders took their farm produce to Ibefun for sale. They trekked in groups, talking and chanting all the way. However, I was to ride with my father on his Raleigh bicycle. What a luxury! I enjoyed that privilege. This was my first trip out of my village. It took us a short time to cover.

On our way, we used the services of our local boat to cross our village river, the OjuAaye. No money was demanded from us because we were known. However, strangers and visitors were made to pay their fare of 2p for the ride. Thereafter, we rode on our bicycle. The footpath was narrow and bumpy. On the road sides were acres of kola nuts and cocoa plantations.

This trip was to be a significant and remarkable landmark in my life. It was the first time I had had close contact with my father. I smelt his sweat and inhaled his breath. Life has a way of sending its messages. Throughout the journey there was only unspoken communication between us; eyes and body language. Not a word was spoken.

Ibefun was a growing town with many beautiful houses, quite different from my village. The women dressed well and looked presentable, unlike my village, where many women preferred going around topless. The law from land to land is different.

The whole family was happy to see us. My brother was very excited. As for me, I was not disappointed at the warm welcome received, having travelled in expectation.

In 1958, after my mother's death, my brother was taken away from the village to live with my father's second wife in Ibefun. She was a quiet and respectable woman from a very wealthy family. Her father, Pa Ologbon Ori, was a very rich and successful merchant in the land. He was famous and known by all and sundry, and massively rich and respected. Pa Ologbon Ori owned the first penthouse in the land. He was the Chief Trustee and Patron of Saint Saviour's Church. Every member of his household was actively involved in church activities.

I would like to mention here that St. Saviours Church had under its management the community Modern School, Holy Trinity, Ibefun-Ilado. The School Principal was Pa Ologbon Ori's nephew. He was cool headed and smart; very respectful and polite. He visited us very often. By the time I arrived, my sister Ore was already attending the Modern School. My brother Israel Ope was not far behind her.

Pa Ologbon Ori's first born was my first stepmother. Her name was Hannah Iyalode (Iya Ore). She was a popular seamstress, widely known and recognised outside her territory. In 1958, her tailoring studio housed over twenty female trainees at a session. She was ahead of all competitors. Hannah Iyalode, Mama Ore was widely known and had two female children for my father, Josephine Ore and Lydia

Adetutu. So into this extended family my brother Israel Ope was absorbed immediately after my mother's death. In the course of time I was to join him.

From that moment on my life changed for good. Now I was amongst people who accepted me. I was instantly absorbed into the family without any prejudice. My frustration was gone and the moody surroundings evaporated. My sisters introduced me to those around the household, including tailoring trainees and the oldest woman in the company, Iya Ekutu, Baba Ologbon Ori's sister. She was very old, wrinkled and bent over with age.

Baba Ologbon Ori ordered a bowl of fried plantain for me. He gave me a nickname, Jebejebe, meaning smart child. It was befitting as I was the youngest, the darling bud of the family.

At Ibefun my life blossomed. I had a father, a mother, siblings and extended family who accepted me without any reservation. My home was happy within, and without my adversaries. There was no hiding, looking back or running from haters, no more discrimination or discouragement from ignorant persecutors. I was not struggling to be loved; no fear chasing me. I was unconditionally free. At Ibefun, I was lifted up by the ability of those around me.

I would love to describe my first stepmother, Hannah Iyalode (Mama Ore). As mentioned previously, she was from a wealthy and influential family, comfortable in her own right. She was brilliant and graceful, simply to be seen. She was kind to me and my brother, and also very sensitive. A totally and completely awesome woman, extremely tender and warm. She cared for me and my brother, and I made sure that we fully paid her back fifty years later. In life, whatever you sow, you eventually reap. Hannah Iyalode reaped hers later in life, to the envy of all women. In my entire life of three score and almost ten years, I have never met another human being like Mama Ore. Throughout the period of my stay and beyond, I never saw her angry, always gentle. She never engaged in fighting anyone. Her posture to me was of meekness and majesty.

I cannot recollect which month of the year it was when I arrived at Ologbon Ori's compound, but it was during school term. Every morning at 7 am, my sisters and brother left for the nearby Catholic Primary School in the company of other neighbourhood children. All my cries to allow me to join the entourage fell on deaf ears. Many excuses were given to me, but one left me confused. I was told to be patient and to wait until my right arm, when stretched across my head, was long enough to touch my left ear! That was a language I did not understand. What a lame excuse. Anyway, help and assurance was always around as Iya Ekutu would draw me into her room to sleep on her mat. Her room was always dark and relaxing, with one unopened window. Her door curtain was a mat. There were baked clay pots for water, and the cooking pots and plates were also of clay; no cutlery. There was no need for that, as food was consumed using our fingers and thumbs. Food tastes better this way.

She would comfort me by narrating how as the best teacher she lectured the so-called primary school teachers, teaching them all they knew. She was able to convince me that all the school teachers attended her classes every evening (when I was fast asleep) and that was why I never saw them! She was so convincing, and I believed her.

Iya Ekutu encouraged me to "help my hands grow longer" by giving me chores to do. I would volunteer to clean, dust her room and rub her walls with goat dung. Sometimes we do stupid things innocently. But she was the best granny any child could wish for. She was always friendly and would point me out to friends and family as her favourite grandchild. She was always around and behind me. She encouraged me to wrestle with my sisters only when she was around, and she would hold down my opponent for me to mount. She was always the judge and cheerer, and with her in my corner I never lost a match. She had a great sense of humour.

One sunny afternoon, I escorted my friends to sell fruits. We roamed around the town with our wares delicately balanced on our heads. Then a woman called us in to buy some oranges. As soon as we entered her house, I recognised her as my mother's relative. I kept my cool, did not say a word. Suddenly, she stared into my eyes, drew me closer to her, turned me round for thorough observation, then slowly said my name - 'Funmilayo?'. I answered back affirmatively. Suddenly, Mama Billy, as she was popularly known, went berserk, burst out screaming and calling the names of her ancestors, begging them to come down and aid her in fighting a common enemy – Mawobe, my father. Mama Billy was unstoppable and uncontrollable.

By now, her husband and two daughters Billy and Muiba, had rushed in to see what the commotion was about. All her neighbours raced in, to rescue her from the so-called enemy. She lifted me off my feet, carried me on her back, tied her wrapper round me to hold me firm and close to her. I was perplexed.

After a while, she told her story. Apparently when my mother and I were sick and in confinement, my mother's family were not allowed to visit us. They were branded witches and sorcerers and accused of many atrocities. They were tormented. The greatest deliverance you can have in life is deliverance from your own people. My father bluntly refused to talk to their emissaries and representatives. Even my mother's death was secretly kept from her family members. My father and his mother made sure that my mother's family was broken in the right and the wrong places. They could not mourn their late sister as they were not even sure of her death. They stretched and struggled but did not succeed; they were held back and down for lack of any news. The entire family was under pressure and provocation. Whatever information they had was rumour. They had no choice but to wait patiently till something concrete was revealed. That is still the situation now.

Her husband wisely advised her that if she wanted the truth, she should go to the source, go and see Mawobe. So, with me still on her back, she rushed out of her house to pay my father a visit. It was time to set the record straight.

My father was sitting comfortably in his armchair when Mama Billy stormed in. Without mincing words, she demanded to know the truth about what had really happened to my mother. Fearlessly, she told my father that she would be visiting her extended family members to broadcast the news that I was living in Ibefun, where my father had been hiding me. There was tension and frustration in the air around.

My father did owe them the truth, but she did not make it easy for him to share it. Sometimes when our emotions are involved, it is difficult to see things as they really are. Lots of explanations and regrets were rendered by my father, but he received only one answer from her. She was coming back the following day with all her family members. My father was warned to be ready for war. She raged off just as she had thundered in, promising to finish the war which my father had started.

On hearing the commotion, Baba Ologbon Ori summoned my father. On hearing his version, the Stateman blamed my father for being very inconsiderate and harsh towards his in-laws. He condemned his actions profusely. Then calmly, Baba Ologbon Ori said something positive would come out of this situation. He advised my father to prostrate himself before his in-laws as soon as they arrived and to plead with them. When you have been around enemies so long, you do not recognise friends.

The following morning, a throng of angry visitors were in Baba Ologbon Ori's compound. Leading them was my mother's eldest sister, Mama Ajoke. She had two children, Abel (deceased) and Ajoke. Ajoke, her daughter, was married to Ogunbase and they had two sons (Afolabi and Adewale) and a daughter named Ajiun. Ajiun was an ebony of beauty.

Mama Ajoke was boiling with rage and spitting venom. Determination to devour my father was written on their faces. She looked back, bent, wobbling, tired and sick. She raged for war and vengeance.

Baba Ologbon Ori came down to welcome them. He called my father out to welcome his in-laws. I positioned myself resting on the door; I was frightened and withdrawn.

The elderly man explained to the meeting that his position was very difficult and delicate. Firstly, my father was a visitor in his house and secondly, he was also his in-law. Finally, he pleaded with them to have respect and honour for his grey hair. Therefore he asked them to be lenient in whatever action they had in mind.

Sooner or later, the hatred in a man's heart finds its way into his words, his heart and eventually into his actions. That was the exact situation when they started narrating their ordeals. My father stood no chance of winning. He just took the advice of the wise man, prostrating himself before his in-laws and begging forgiveness. Whilst the wailing, screaming and abusive language was going on, at intervals, Baba Ologbon Ori asked for patience and consideration.

Mama Ajoke thanked Baba Ologbon Ori for his patience and wisdom. Furthermore, she said that she regarded him as a respectable and outstanding community elder. However, she said that her faith in humanity had taken a bit of battering lately because my father had allowed death to take away the star in her family. With tears rolling down her cheeks, she openly and defiantly said 'A naked man fears no pickpocket,' meaning that she has nothing to lose any more since she has lost all.

Baba Ologbon Ori, looking slightly towards me, advised both parties to let go of their bitterness, revenge and hatred for the sake of the little girl in their midst as parenthood was the balance between softness and strength. He appeased everyone's spirit by calmly saying "Out of the ashes of what we have left will arise what we have lost. The dry remnant of a garden flower will blossom one day if nurtured with love and care". This moved everybody to tears, including my father.

To Mama Ajoke, the wise man said, "You do not have to be in prison doing time. You are punishing yourself because you felt you let your junior sister down as you were not there when she needed you most". He got up from his chair and held her tightly. Shaking and rocking her lightly, he gave her an assurance that her spirit was there with her even to the end. Lastly, he advised the two sides to get together, encouraging them to get along with one another.

I was happy that the task of choosing between my father and my mother's family was not thrown at me, because there was no debate in my mind about it. The hardest choices are those closest to your heart. Out of pity and love, I would have gone with my mother's family. They were all emotional wrecks and crying. Their loss was too much for them to bear, and seeing me standing there was the only consolation for them.

Life is wonderful. For the brief time I became alive at Ibefun, I forgot my dark and gruesome past; I felt alive there. My next move belonged to fate.

Chapter 6

RETURN TO HOME BASE

I never knew that it was customary for my family to have Christmas and New Year celebrations together in our ancestral house. Because most of my childhood had been spent in isolation, I did not know that this annual get-together was idolised in the family.

Our entourage, comprising my brother, two sisters and myself, was led by my first stepmother. We left Ibefun in the evening of Christmas Eve, arriving at Eyinwa within the hour. We were very playful on our way, pulling grass and throwing stones at squirrels and anything that moved. As evening came, we arrived at the river bank and had a smooth crossing.

We were still far away when we saw the crowd coming to welcome us. The welcome party was for Mama Ore. Greetings were exchanged in traditional ways, the young men prostrating themselves to the elders and little girls kneeling in submission. For a brief moment, I felt the past chasing and catching up on me. I withdrew to a corner; my feelings did not really matter. What reality was I living in now? My past or my present? I thought my old self had been drowned.

Just then, from nowhere, came a voice from the past calling my name. Looking up at once, there she was standing right there in front of me, my nurse. I rushed into her arms. She lifted me up and crushed me to her chest. "What are you doing here?" was my first greeting to her and "when did you arrive?" was my second. She answered that she had arrived about two months ago and had now been bestowed on my father as his new wife. I remembered that that had been my mother's request of her before she died. She was entrusted with a mission to take care of me. She was now married to my father and living in our house, taking over my mother's room.

She told me that whatever you yield yourself to in life is what you become. She obeyed my dying mother's instructions. Our words outlive and outlast us. She is now my second stepmother and no longer my nurse. Nature has a way of manoeuvring people.

I could not recollect any introductions between my two stepmothers. Apparently they already knew of each other's existence and position. The senior wife, if jealous, was not showing it. Her feelings did not control her. That was awesome maturity. She immediately gave her junior a nickname, 'Oloruko', meaning 'namesake', as she shared the same name with my paternal grandmother. It is an insult to call your elders by name, so nicknames are given to show respect to relatives bearing the same names.

Our house was full of well-wishers welcoming us back home and congratulating my father on taking a new wife. Also, I noticed that there was a very big lantern light in our yard which drew people and insects in. My father's small battery-operated 'TYPE' radio was blaring away news in local languages. There was merrymaking and happiness in the air. A good night's sleep was well deserved.

The following day was Saturday. Very early in the morning, we were given our chores by the senior wife. Mine was to sweep the courtyard and later to fetch water from the stream. I loved every minute of it.

My new stepmother prepared a special bath for me. She took care in examining my scars and bending my limbs and fingers. She was asking many questions about my skin sensitivity. From the onset, I was warned not to bathe in the stream as my skin had not healed enough. Neither was I to use soda soap, as it was deemed too harsh for my scars. A blend of palm and coconut oils would sooth me. She gave me a nickname, 'Abeke', meaning a child you cajole and beg to pamper.

Late that morning we made a trip to our ancestral house. Everyone was present. My paternal grandmother was a good hostess and looked proud of her close-knit family. My Uncle Robert and his wife returned home from Lagos, and we were welcomed with salutations and greetings. The atmosphere was filled with the aroma of cooked meals, and there was plenty to eat. Amidst the noisy greetings and chatting, food was served by the women. All the grandchildren were served first, followed by our parents and other elders present.

By nature, I am a straightforward person and any answerable question thrown at me receives a straight answer. So when asked by my grandmother if I had returned to live with her, my answer was not mixed - no way.

As the head of the family, my father made a marriage announcement. There was to be a new wife in the family. My Uncle Isaac was to take a new bride. The formal family introduction had taken place early in October, but the final ceremony was planned to coincide with end-of-year homecomings. There was no objection, but no excitement either. Something was not right. Though his wife, Opelenge (the slimming one), was present during the announcement, she was dignified and quiet. Her womb might be barren, but she was not barren of pride.

After that first home visit, our visits became more regular. Preparations were made for the arrival of the new family addition – a new wife for my Uncle Isaac.

As custom demands, the bride would be escorted to her groom's house in the evening amidst dancing and merrymaking. Singers and dancers would be praising her and her family and assuring her that she had made the right choice. They would pray to all the deities to bless her womb so that she would have nine boys and a girl to cradle.

Early in that Saturday morning in December 1959, I accompanied my new stepmother as we left for our ancestral house so as to help my grandmother with cooking and other preparations. My grandmother cooked her favourite dish, ikokore (grated water yams seasoned with herbs and smoked tiger prawns), happily boasting that this dish puts her name on the community catering services. It's a family thing.

Prior to our arrival, work had almost been completed by well-wishers and extended family members. However, we found our place and followed in line of preparations. We anxiously awaited the arrival of the bride, and when she eventually came, I had the greatest shock of my life. It was none other than my dear confidant and friend Tinuade. I was spellbound, speechless. When eventually I found my tongue, my greetings to her were in questions: "What are you doing here? Are you the new wife? But I thought you were my friend? So, you will be living here now?" All the questions came rushing out.

She calmly called me aside and explained to me that we would be holding a 'head-to-head' talk the following day and for now I should just enjoy the ceremony. I waited, doing nothing; and sometimes doing nothing is something.

Tinuade was well adorned and her presentation was absolutely sensational. She wore a native dress made of green and yellow damask material. Her earrings were of leaf pattern. Twisted around her neck was a thick golden chain with a large pendant bearing a pattern of a dropping leaf. It was a thing of beauty. She carried a small beaded bag suspended from her fingers. She looked fresh and charming. Was she beautiful? Yes, Tinuade was very beautiful.

The bridal room was well decorated with woven curtain materials; there were piles of native woven clothes on the bed and a carved sitting stool positioned beside the bed. The room invited you in. Oh what an evening! The rest of the evening dragged on into the early hours of Sunday morning.

It was long after the wedding ceremony before Tinuade and I had time to talk, as she promised. She had been bestowed to my uncle and had accepted his hand in marriage just because of me. She wanted me to know that her future in my family depended greatly on my cooperation, because whilst the present mattered, the future mattered most. Furthermore, she said that there were bound to be huge changes in the family, so it was important to be prepared for the forthcoming reforms. She hoped to have all her children in our family, but made me promise that I would help raise them. She believed that I would find myself in a flourishing environment. The future she said, belongs to those who have foresight. All her explanations made me more confused.

The marriage was blessed with the birth of a firstborn, a son, Abimbola, thus bringing happiness to the marriage and good luck to the home. In all, the family had seven beautiful children, both boys and girls. They were adorable kids.

When the children started coming, my Uncle Isaac began to diminish both in wealth and position. Having children started to give him pain. According to a reliable family source, the Deity had foretold that he would only become a father in life if he gave up his affluence and wealth. He had no option but to choose fertility. Though he lost his worldly values, his children were his joy and love of his life.

My Uncle Isaac was a doting, dutiful father and husband. His triumph came out of his troubles at last. He died in 1979, leaving behind his wife Tinuade and seven wonderful, smart and stunning children. He was given a befitting princely burial. His wife continually reminded me of my promise in raising the kids.

Unknown to many people, the cord of friendship between me and Tinuade was extended to her children. I love them all like my own. The first born was pampered with affection by all. He was very close to me; he was of thoughtful character and full of true emotions. He was loveable.

Some of the children were living with me from an early age. Their mother was never far away from me and we raised them all together. They are not my relatives. They are more than that; they are flesh of my flesh and the bone of my bone. They are all very close to me, closer than they will ever know.

My second stepmother was very persuasive; she convinced me that I should stay behind after the Christmas and New Year celebrations. She listened carefully to me and said that happiness was already within me and I just needed to remove my worries to reveal it. Her words were beyond argument, and I agreed with her.

I started my education at St. Paul's Primary School, Eyinwa, in 1959. This was a new me. I quickly shed off my fears and intimidation, focusing on my new life and education. The ordeals of the past strengthened my determination to succeed. This time around, village life was more enjoyable and less painful. My stepmother was there to guide me. Sometimes you win because of who is watching. She believed that I could do it, and she was right. I had a dutiful primary school teacher,

Mr Matthew Otusanya, and a disciplinarian Headmaster, Mr J K Oshinaike. My future lived in the educational foundation and background which they built for me. They practised thorough teaching and dedication to duty. God bless their work and efforts on my behalf.

Preparations for Nigeria's independence were followed by lavish cultural displays and acrobatic dances. All the masquerades, namely Okoro, Epa, Jigbo, Agere and Egungun, paraded at the Empire & Independence Day fairs. The masquerades' masks were stunningly adorned with colours and they would speak to you; their beautiful colours said it all. The Independence Day Parade was a multitude of pleasures, with a great response and applause from the crowd who gathered to cheer right from the beginning to the end. The Independence Ceremony touched the heart of the whole nation; there was an enormous feeling of a great event going on. The crowd went wild watching the astonishing show. It was a superb performance. While the old danced, the young were dreaming.

We ordinary people made a big difference on Independence Day. We all were given cups, caps and flags to wave at parades. Oh what a day! A big brother who participated in the activities and witnessed it all is still very much around. His name is Deinji. His acrobatic skills were exceptionally entertaining. If asked, he would relay every moment. His brain holds records of a vanished cultural past. Deinji's interest in cultural activities is age defying and unquenchable. Whenever he sings, rendering the traditional melodies, and playing the traditional flutes, his playful spirit lifts our hearts up. Deinji is a real live wire. I personally find his music eccentric and electric. He has sensitive ears for music. He would postpone his own wedding night for a masquerade outing. He was born a tradition fanatic. Personally I adore him. He is a soft nut.

Eyinwa is famously known as the Village of Culture. Elders are always looking at environmental issues, settling disputes and allocating farmland to newcomers and migrants who want to establish themselves. Collectively as a community we are strong, strict and possibly stubborn. We do not get down on our knees too readily. Our traditional music is addictively good and pleasant. Dancing glues us together.

Every position has its own pains. This was true of my second stepmother. She was reported by some people who accused her of ill-treating me. They complained that hawking and chores were stealing my childhood, but they were just building wild rumours about her reputation. Leaving her behind really pained my heart, but she advised me to see the goodness in every opportunity.

Chapter 7

A NEW DAWN

So in January 1963, I left my village with my most senior brother and followed him to Lagos. It was a move to make a fresh start in a new place, with new people and fresh opportunities. It was a land of progress and opportunities for great adventures in life. Lagos is a strong economic city.

We lived in the Mainland area of Lagos in Willoughby Street. This happened to be one of the affluent middle-class areas in the city. I was enlisted into New Era Primary School, Standard 3. Shortly after, I moved to St Jude's Primary School, Ebute

Metta, the most popular and prosperous school in Lagos. It was headed by Mr Odugbose, who was an eagle-eyed Headmaster, and nothing escaped his notice. He was a strict disciplinarian, all in the cause of education. It was a privilege to study there. There is an existing relationship between the Primary School and St Jude's Church.

I was in Lagos, the magnificent capital of Nigeria, when the Nigerian Civil War began. The war affected us in different ways. The only uniformed personnel ever seen around was the police force, only effective in collecting taxes from unwilling farmers, traders and dodgers. We never saw soldiers around before then. They were kept in their barracks. With their arrival came road checks and blocks. We were warned not to speak at all to them or to strangers (every wall has ears and eyes); it was a tough time to be young in Nigeria, with not many opportunities around.

Tight security measures were introduced by the Nigerian Federal Military Government and many slogans emerged; "No careless talk", "Join the Civil Defence"; "Nigeria is for All of You"; "Don't sit on the fence, Join the Civil Defence". A slogan was carved based on the President's name: "Go On With One Nigeria – GOWON". The name you give a child goes before him in life and honour and dignity is in the name. General Yakubu Gowon's name was a beacon of continuity. He was a symbol of unrivalled power and influence. General Gowon just happened to stumble into the place of destiny. From a human perspective, this slogan encouraged many people. It ignited our unity flame and it is still burning and keeping us together now. He soldiered on like the military man he was.

Major General Yakubu Gowon, a symbolic figure, was sworn in in 1966 as the Military Head of State, the supreme leader of his age. At 31 years of age he was the most eligible bachelor in Nigeria. He fell in love with a maiden, Victoria, who was a nurse by profession. She was tall, beautiful and fascinating to look at.

I was lucky to have secondary admission offers from two secondary schools. Life is a series of choices that lead us to our destiny. My choice of a Catholic school was the best.

I started my secondary school education in January 1966 during the civil war. My college, Our Lady of Apostles Secondary School, was one of the best Catholic schools in Nigeria. For the first time in my life, I was exposed to another form of Christian ideology and worship modes, bible teachings and explanations, understanding, and participation. This was a new ground, limelight and exposure. This was a training ground for me to learn new principles and meditation. Immediately on admission to the college, I felt myself being brought to my mission and led to my position. I was surrounded by innocent school mates, with a sense of joy, happiness, and gratitude.

All my teachers and mates knew me for my craving for religion knowledge, worship and activities. My biblical interpretations were on a higher ground than those of my class. In my second year at college, I was chosen to be the School Bell Bearer/Ringer notifying all of the ends of class sessions, prayer times (Angelus), study times and worship times. Worshipping whets and quenches my spiritual thirst. The yearning for God, my thirst for gladness and happiness, was satisfied in worship praising God. My secondary school education at Our Lady of Apostles Catholic School was my period of spiritual confirmation and transformation. I was being moved gradually and systematically towards my destiny.

I knew then that my life was significant and that I did have a role to play. Even my mates foresaw me going into discipleship, legions or a convent. God calls us out of whom people call us. God was shaping me into position.

With the escalation of the civil war and the advance of the Biafran Army on Ore and Benin, we were all sceptical of the outcome. My college, Our Lady of Apostles Secondary School, is situated close to the border of Midwest and Western Nigeria. Every dawn, we would see trailer-loads of soldiers being driven towards Ore and the battle front. The soldiers were most of the time singing aloud of their determination to slaughter their enemies. They had various war slogans.

We would peep from our dormitory windows to see what was going on outside (although we were forbidden to do so) while lying on our beds, and hiding under our blankets, praying fervently for safety and protection. The atmosphere was gripping and nail-biting as the violence escalated.

According to news received, many Nigerian soldiers were overwhelmed by the rebels and were being slaughtered in Ore by the Biafran Army. The young soldiers had not been fully taught the art of war. But Nigeria fought back savagely and the battle was intense. Ore saw the bloodiest battle of the civil war. The slaughter there turned the River Niger red with human blood. It saw the hottest and harshest fight, but was later liberated.

There was bloodshed and brutality all around. The Easterners (Ibos) living in Lagos were terrorised as a result of the Casino Cinema House bombing. Ibos and Yorubas, who had lived together side by side in harmony, were driven apart.

Tension grew amongst neighbours and atrocities were committed against civilians. Both sides committed appalling atrocities. Events took a violent turn in the northern parts of Nigeria, with murdering and torturing.

Some people are religious to the point of missing realities and revelations, but our Principal, Sister John, was not one of them. She was very observant and sensible. She was put in that strategic position to help us. She protected us, and all the Ibo girls were shielded.

One early morning in March 1967, at the school assembly, Sister John announced that due to the warfare the school was having to close. Sometimes you need to do something radical, but she dismissed the students without the consent of the School Governors.

A crisis requires a resolution. She told the Assembly that it was solely her decision to temporarily close the school for the sake of everyone. However, as she did not wait for the unanimous decision of the School Governors, she would have to bear the brunt should her decision be overruled. What do you do when your right is wrong? You see, power is all right until you become a victim of someone else's power. As our School Principal, she was administratively in control of the school, but for major decisions such as a school closure, the School Governors reigned supreme. She surely must have considered the potential damage to her career before making the decision, but on the whole Sister John used her discretion; she was persuaded by her own mind. She displayed a sense of responsibility and accountability.

On instinct, and for safety's sake, I decided to return to my village instead of travelling to Lagos because the possibility of air raids over Lagos was very high. My father and stepmother were not surprised to see me, as they too had been listening to locally transmitted news on their battery-operated TYPE radio. The news of an air raid and bombing of a local cinema house at Ebute-Metta was still fresh on everyone's mind.

Chapter 8

CASUALTIES AND BRUTALITIES

On my second day at home, my stepmother called me aside to break some sad news. She told me that Alonje, the local palm wine tapper, was dead. His death made the village suspicious. The story had it that one of the local neighbouring tribal rulers had died and according to tradition, he should not be buried alone. Tradition had it that when a ruler passes away, as it is a long journey to the after-life, he should be accompanied by servants and where possible wives to keep him company. This is terrifying. So, the community elders decided to give their departed chief a fitting burial by lining his grave with an entourage. They carefully planned their calculated attacks, and unfortunately Alonje was a victim.

According to information, Alonje was lured into heavy drinking by his assailants. He drank himself to oblivion (so they thought). In life, the very gift that nature gives you may be the one that ends you, but a bit of caution will not kill you.

By the time he realised that this was a lethal setup, it was too late. He was a lone ranger amongst a group of able-bodied hackers. Alonje's death was agonisingly painful.

However, there was a dark side of Alonje's life that only a few people knew. He was the head of a divinity secret society and a master orator and diviner. There is a great difference between our actual selves and our spiritual selves. It is not the position that a man occupies that matters but the power within him. His attackers got the wrong person on their deadly mission.

Knowing fully well that he was trapped and at a point of no return, Alonje begged his assailants to let him urinate. He was allowed to do so. What do you do when you are a captive in a situation over which you have no control? Alonje defended himself. Alone in the corner, he bent down, digging his fingers into the soft sand. Then he took two handfuls of sand, uttered some incantations and sprayed all his attackers with the sand - psychological manipulation. They struck him dead. It was a bloody and brutal death and he was never seen again; his body was never found. This part of our culture is approaching barbarism. Have we lost the culture war?

Some days after the incident, two of the attackers became sick and died within hours. The same thing happened to another young man who was present at Alonje's ordeal. He died within a day of boils and rashes. After the death of a fifth man, the village elders grew suspicious and the attackers confessed their crime. Only then did they realise that they had bitten off more than they could chew. They had created the crisis themselves and nobody could help them.

Alonje's character was revealed in his final hour and he had defended himself by the only means he knew. You never discover what is inside you if you do not have something challenging you. You do not know how strong you are until you are attacked. Alonje used his wits, his faculties and his common sense. He fought for his life even when he was losing it. Alonje placed a curse on all of them. They all died, fifteen men, within a month. It was a case of a life for a life. Be careful who speaks into your life.

With this evil practice in our modern world, we are a culture going down. Acts like this have made us go down morally and disgracefully, making us the seeds of evildoers. Let us pray for moral awakening, because morality foundation is culture. If lessons could be learnt from Alonje's death, and if our joint voices could proclaim the message of being our brothers' keepers, then we can claim victory by his loss. We learn the value of things when you lose them.

I grieved for Alonje, because he had taken good care of me when I was sick. He was my wine tapper, my story teller, my cheerful and chatty friend. I found him intelligent and genuinely funny. He taught me the act of smooth-sipping palm wine. Ours was a profound friendship on a personal and professional level.

Things were not going well in the east. Biafra was facing defeat. As the civil war drew to an end, the Federal Government got the upper hand. Biafran pride was greatly dented by the defeat and loss of the war. The conquest of major eastern cities like Enugu and Onitsha was the climax of the war. Such innocent bloodshed was necessary to get us to where we are today.

The Federal Military Government of Nigeria swallowed Biafra. Biafra was doomed. The fighting stopped; the destructive war was over. Defeat destroyed the Biafran Republic. There is a just God who presides over the destiny of nations.

Eventually our school resumed and studies continued. New subjects were added to the school syllabus, amongst which were the Latin and French languages. I discovered that I had an undiscovered talent for languages.

Finally, my secondary education ended in 1970 and I came out with good grades. Shortly afterwards, my senior brother lost his wife, so I was told, leaving me with my two-year-old niece to nurse. So for a period, I was housebound and taking care of my immediate family.

The Federal Government awarded me a scholarship to study as a stenographer at the Federal Training Centre in Lagos. With further training and certificates from Pitman's College in London, I qualified as a Confidential Secretary in 1973.

As fate would have it, I met and got married to the first man in my life in 1973, even though my father did not approve of the union. I was a virgin wife. That should not surprise anyone. My education and my scrutinised background were responsible for my innocent, overblown, imaginative and romantic mind.

My new husband was an army officer and his duty calls took me to various places between 1973 and 1975. I was in Calabar, Port Harcourt and Uyo, all in South East Nigeria, and Ile-Ife, the cradle of the Yorubas. The marriage was blessed with a son in 1976.

My circle of friends and associates changed to people from the high ruling class. I had high hopes and expectations for my marriage, but though we were together, we were not the same. What do you do when what you expected to work fails to do so? He turned out to be a cheat, a wife beater and an unappreciative man. He was being groomed for a state governorship post, but it went away all so quickly and he achieved little fame. He completely lost it. Some good words of advice were given, but he did not heed them. He recklessly chose concubines and repeatedly lied about being seduced by witchcraft. Moreover, he claimed that women used their looks and lures as tools on him. He was trying different version of his tactics. He was controlling, manipulative and sneaky.

As time went on his behaviour became scandalous and deeply offensive. His weakness encouraged waywardness amongst his subordinates and officers alike. He woefully failed the real test of how to handle power. He became power drunk; he was in office but not in power. His accomplices accused their fancy women of using pillow talk to influence their official regimental decisions. They were all partners in crime. What a dangerous alliance against authority!

So my husband's ambition as a soldier came to nothing and his life of luxury and privilege was torn from him. In an extraordinary turn of events, he was officially court-martialled by the Army. All accusations against him were proved and had permanent consequences for him. The truth has the bad habit of coming out. He was found guilty by the Nigerian Armed Forces and eventually he lost everything, including his army career.

In 1977, after four years of turbulent marriage, the relationship collapsed completely; divorce was looming. So I left with my child Dare and moved back to Lagos, where I found myself hunted by his greyhounds. He chased me because he thought he owned me, but he was wrong. IN 1978, blinded by pure revenge, hatred and jealousy and amidst terrible threats, he abducted our child, and there was no help from my family. That was the saddest and most humiliating period of my life.

My father and eldest brother said to my face that I deserved all I got because I had not heeded their warnings. I was deeply disappointed by their attitude towards me. This unresolved disappointment led to frustration, because in the past I had devoted my time and energy to them. In fact I devoted my life to supporting my immediate family, but in time of crisis they backed off. The ensuing conflicts between us were devastating. There was tension in the family which broke into open conflict. I felt abused by my spouse and used by my family, who openly mocked me. I felt unloved again.

All these trials, tribulations and frustrations pushed me into suicidal temptations. I was battling with forces known and unknown; lightning, storms, quakes and floods of life and overwhelming opposition everywhere. In the face of compelling evidence, I was still rejected. I cannot remember what they said word for word but I remember how they made me feel. What a life!

When you are in a hole, you stop digging. Anyhow, one has to forgive and release bitterness. There is no pain greater than the pain you are related to. I did not want to put my feelings on public display, so I bottled them all up within myself with a yearning determination to put them all to shame once I succeeded. There was invisible purpose in my pains; my life would explode with blessings. I was more than the person they saw.

I had to rely on my inner strength to fight and defeat my adversaries. There was anxiety in the midst of uncertainty, but I resisted my own fears and their condemnation. Life can be a misery. The people you help most kick you hardest, and the most hateful are the ones you try to help.

Chapter 9

APPRECIATING GOODNESS IN OTHERS

With my secretarial education, I was able to hold gainful employment as a confidential secretary with renowned and reputable companies like the University of Ife, Nestle Foods and West African Portland Cement. I met some very good and reliable friends and workmates. One of them was Olori Bola Otegbeye. She continues to be a friend in need and indeed. We met in 1981, living as next door neighbours in Mafoluku, an area close to Muritala Muhammed International Airport, where Bola was the Assistant Public Relations Manager. Ours is a predestined friendship. We stood together through thick and thin. We were both running away not only from families and foes but also from woeful marriages. I am glad that I picked her as a friend, because she has contributed more to my destiny than any other friend. We survived on bread and water and it was a hard life. Bola was always advising and encouraging me not to allow myself to go into depression over a temporary situation. You do not need anything you lost to bless you. I am happy that I listened to her advice.

One Saturday in 1986, packing and loading my car with some food and bottles of wine, I travelled home to my village, Eyinwa. It was evening time when we arrived. I drove straight to the house of Baba Otusanya and found him sitting delicately on his bed; old and fragile he looked. I was given a warm welcome by everyone. The whole house was full of his children, grandchildren and great grandchildren. Baba Otusanya was blessed at his old age and surrounded by his own.

On entering the room, I announced my arrival. I sat beside him and introduced myself. His eyes were dimmed with age and he could not recognise me. Anyway, I explained my mission, recalling all his visits to us in the secluded hut, the herbs and medications, the incantations and palm wine liberations.

Suddenly, Baba Otusanya gathered himself together, drew his covering clothes to himself and then with all the strength and air left within him and his lungs, let out loud and deafening screams. His whole body was shaking. Everybody present was astonished. Then he tearfully said, "Oh! God has kept me alive to see this day and to reap the fruit of my labour!" He stretched his hands and with the tips of his fingers he touched my face and forehead. He felt the scars on the backs of my hands. It was as if he was looking for the Scars of Affectionate Memories. If you really want to know about me, look around you. I am what you are seeing; scarred, bruised, jilted, dented but loved and cherished. I have all it takes to be me - a human being.

He called me by my native name and I answered. Then, with a wave of his hands, he drew everyone's attention to himself. He said that in 1953 to 1956, I had been a small defenceless child and he had been a very strong and active man. Now, thirty years later, when he was weak and defenceless, I had returned to repay him for all that he had done. He said this was the day of reckoning and God had kept him alive to reap and taste what he had brewed. With stern warning, he gave an advisory talk to his household to always do good.

After presenting the food and wine, I handed him an envelope, gave him a hug and left. That was the last time I saw Baba Otusanya, because he died a few months afterwards. At his funeral, I had my own circle of friends to honour the dead and we gave Baba Otusanya a fitting burial.

The present Village Traditional Ruler, Baale Kolawole Otunsanya, is my cousin, the only child of my mother's sister – Adebimpe Odusanya, born to Baba Otunsanya.

Baba Awofala died when I was in Calabar. I did not receive any news from home regarding his death. To show my gratitude for his love and care to my mother and myself, I wrote a personal thank you letter to his first child, Madam Urajo Awofala, stating all the assistance her father had given to us in 1953-1957. I also enclosed substantial gifts. Our characters grow into fruitful trees. Even generations yet unborn reap and eat of the fruits.

My father Mawobe later became our Traditional Ruler. His chieftaincy was approved and confirmed by the Awojale of Ijebuland, Oba Sikiru Adetona, in 1985. His reign was peace on the land. He lived to the ripe old age of 88 years, and he appreciated my loving care towards him.

Abigail Alaba, my nurse-cum-stepmother, died in 1994, similarly swept away like my birth mother. Though childless, Abigail Alaba could not have wished for a better daughter than me. She was brought into my life for a purpose; and she did well. I ensured and saw to it that she enjoyed an extravagant, pampered life.

Chapter 10

MY STRUGGLES AND MANIFESTATIONS

I dabbled a little in Nigerian politics at this time, assisting a friend, as we were determined to return to society the values of the good and free education given to us. During the course, I met the top politicians of my time, Governor Jakande of Lagos State, Governor Ajasin of Ondo State, Governor Bola Ige of Oyo State and most of all Chief Obafemi Awolowo and his wife Chief (Mrs) Awolowo.

Audience with Governor Jakande of Lagos State

Presentation to Chief (Mrs) Obafemi Awolowo

My friend Akin made and released a record in appreciation of the sound education enjoyed in the old Western Region of Nigeria. Our contributions were recognised and appreciated by the ruling parties, leaders and the populace at large. Fortunately for me, I knew when to throw in the towel and back out of politics.

When at the end of 1988 I decided to venture out, I never expected such opposition because I was facing a new life and new hope. My position was comfortable; I had a good job, my own accommodation and young children keeping me company, but there was not much in prospect for the future.

Then, whilst still contemplating in my mind what to do, I received an unexpected visitor. It was on a Saturday, at dawn, that a ghost from my past paid me a visit. Tinuade knocked on my door at dawn to advise me not travel. She got down on her knees crying and begging me not to leave her. After calming down, she said that a visionary had told her of my intended journey and that if I went, it would be for a long time and I would only be returning to Nigeria for holidays. In her own words, "Erelu, you are destined for greatness, we all know that, but also our belief in the power of supernatural must not be underrated".

After much persuasion, she agreed with me that my intended journey was for a brief period, as usual. For many years, I had been travelling abroad for business and holidays and that pattern was not about to change. Her stunning advice to me was to always remember where I came from, as this would make me understand the purpose of my life and who I am.

So for a better tomorrow, I ventured out for greener pastures, leaving behind, with my senior brother, my two innocent and adorable children, Orimoloye and Abisoye. I came to Britain for computer training, investing in myself for a better future. I was thinking that with my secretarial background, there would be greater and better opportunities for my career. Unless you try to do something beyond what you have already mastered, you will never grow. You have to learn beyond your situation.

However, dreams come with trauma. On arrival at Charing Cross, London, I found out that the cousin with whom I had intended to stay had died two weeks earlier. Nobody had contacted us. I was burdened with the task of breaking the bad news to the people back home. Financial aid did not come from Nigeria because the extended family was busy burying the departed in absentia.

My plight took me to a close family friend living not too far from my cousin's flat. Initially, I was welcomed into the family, but not for long. The man of the house, Pastor Ibala, who was the local pastor, decided to try his luck with me. According to him, he found me irresistible. So with my sharp tongue I reminded him that he used to be my driver in Nigeria and with me his position would never change. So because I would not be available, agreeable and accessible, and because of this pastor's ignorance and intolerance, I found myself homeless.

On the other hand, his wife, Nube, could not comprehend what was happening, because I kept quiet about her husband's madness. During conversations, Nube was always referring to all the care and gifts I used to splash out on her and the children while in Nigeria. So when the husband threw me out of their flat, his wife opened her mouth wide with surprise; hers was silent screaming! She was asking me what was happening, but her questions should have been directed to her husband, not me.

Pastor Ibala's behaviour was a grave provocation to me, as I did not expect that from him. I took great care of him, pampering his family with love and gifts when in Nigeria. Pastor Ibala and others like him do not appreciate kindness and will never reciprocate.

Life sometimes disrupts your expectations. As for me, I got used to being disappointed. This vulnerable but determined mind of mine! Though the future was uncertain, I took up my boxes and left. I thank my enemies for displacing me so that I was no longer in their nest. I do not have to do something wrong for people to dislike me.

Progress always comes at a cost and nobody is going to stand in my way. To get my identity I had to be far away from these associates and have a mind that went beyond my situation.

When life hands you something that you do not expect, this is no time to cry – you must run for help. That was what I did. You cannot have a better future without some displacement.

There and then, I was alone – Me, myself and I; missing my Nigerian home. my soft bed and my two cuddly children, but this was not the time to sob. Finding myself in this temporary situation forced me to make some permanent decisions. Firstly, never to worship half-witted clerics, secondly, to move with great and intelligent people, and thirdly, to make my current stop my new start. So thinking fast but acting slowly, I decided that I would be responsible, respectful and resourceful.

There were some hurdles on the way which needed to be jumped. Laying aside pains and avoiding stumbling, I ran with endurance, determined to win.

Chapter 11

CLIMBING A SLIPPERY LADDER

There was a missing link in my life that I needed to find; my child, the son who had been abducted at the tender age of three by his father. I found him through the grapevine. The process was time consuming - an accumulation of boring days – but at the end of the search, despite the avalanche of allegations and accusations made by his father, my son surfaced. Powerful, prayerful words were like bullets fired to change my circumstances. I spoke positively about my circumstances and my guardian angel moved on my behalf. Never underrate the power of silent prayers.

For the first time in my life, I realised that God had endowed me with some spectacular gifts – biblical knowledge, the power of prophesy and His anointing. They became alive. Bending down on my arms and legs, I called on to the Almighty God, Christ the Saviour and Holy Spirit the Comforter, for rescue and restoration beyond imagination. Things started happening. Reminding myself of my mother's predictions on her death bed, and trusting in God to see me through, my heart became bolder within me. I came out stronger.

My journey in life brought me to an adoring family. Finally, I met my soulmate, Hugh. Whatever term you have for it does not matter, as I had found my home far away from home. What a taste of affection and freedom! Good just got better, and the best was yet to come. My life was strengthened by a new lovely alliance.

At a very mature age, I gave birth to a beautiful baby; what a blessing from God! We named her AnuOluwapo, meaning 'God's mercy is in abundance'. From a very tender age, she made us laugh and giggle with joy.

I secured a local government job in Tufnell Park as an audio secretary within the Housing Department. The motivation I received within the team encouraged me to progress and study further, and I eventually

CAPTAIN MOTHER OLUFUNMILAYO HASSON

My new family life with my husband and children

qualified as a Housing Officer. I moved my job closer to home by transferring to Hackney local government in 1992.

However in 1994, there was a wave of racial discrimination – the 'Skin War'; harassment and victimisation against the blacks, especially Africans working in Hackney Council. Immigration checks, stop and search on the streets as well as home visits, were rampant. It was a visible problem; a life of harassment and constant fear. Many workers lost their jobs, and I was no exception.

Those who victimise are modern day oppressors, and victims will never be free until they leave their employment. I could only feel the pains in this post and did not see the purpose of bearing it any longer.

There are things in life that only experience will teach you. Racial discrimination in the workplace is of the highest order and more is hidden than revealed. The Government Equal Opportunities Act does not go far enough. Racial discrimination is a good drowning tool, and sometimes one needs to be attacked by it in order to appreciate the trauma which victims go through. The atmosphere in the workplace was terrifying and explosive. It was a crazy level of discrimination and antagonism. Living with discrimination is not living at all.

The people who were exposed to opportunities (because of their race) but failed to use them were always offended about everything. They had the chances and the opportunities, but they failed to take them. Despite the fact that the local and national newspapers were alerting the authorities to intervene, only a few who had an attack of conscience spoke out against the oppression.

Anyhow, I did not allow what happened to control me. In fact it renewed and hardened my determination to succeed. My determination lifted me up. Despite the setback, I focussed on my mission to succeed. I got another job, in Waltham Forest.

Having secured a good job and accommodation, I brought my kids to the UK from Nigeria. Now our family was complete; ours was the greatest cast ever assembled. This was also a time of great anxiety, for I did not know what the future held for my young family. I bought my first property in England, a three-

From top left: my husband Hugh, Orim, Abi, myself and Rachel

bedroom house in Forest Gate. My preference for this location was influenced by my regular church attendance at Cherubim & Seraphim Church located at Earlham Grove Road, East London. The Lord had previously revealed to me that this church was His Seat and His majestic presence would always be felt there. The Church reflects the spiritual Christian presence in London. The C & S HQ in Earlham Grove Road is the Citadel of God. To me this is the citadel and gateway to Heaven.

I believe that my right to protection is in the House of God. Also, I wanted my young family to be involved in church service and doctrines – after all, the centre of Christianity is in the home. I wanted to connect my kids with their spiritual life, because spiritual intercession will not work with the ignorant mind. I am a spiritual being, and my spirit only rests when I am in my purpose. If introducing them into spiritualism at an early age was risky, then that was a risk I was prepared to take; with no risk, there is no reward. God loves risk-takers. I believed that that the best way for my children to learn to know God was through me and my commitment, and not through the computer. Intimacy with God is knowing Him intimately. So I gave my children time, and loved putting responsibility into them.

Life was uniquely at ease for me when I started attending the church. I never expected victimisation or envy in the House of God. I was innocently stupid, thinking all who call the name of the Lord and God are His children. How wrong I was. The greater percentage of worshippers is on the offside; the good are few in number. Envy, backbiting and controversy are the order of the day at the grassroots. In their midst, I was as blind as a bat. My accusers were rooted to the Church, but not to God in Christ. When eventually my eyelids were opened and I stood up to defend myself, my accusers could not find anything wrong against me; the gang leader had invented it all. What a prominent and provocative character!

The Holy Bible, which contains the rules of God on earth, became my companion. God speaks out to us through the Holy Bible. I threw myself into serious study for strong spiritual prowess; I did not back down. I am a scholar. The Word of God regenerates and gives confidence. God rescued me from the clutches of haters and stalkers for a purpose, and I must fulfil it.

When God wants to move, He uses one good person. I was raised in the House of God, but nothing prepared me for the persecutions I went through at this headquarters. God sent persecutions to shake me out of my comfort zone. I do not blame my persecutors, as God used them to wake me up.

While the oppressors were fighting for power and identity, I saw my direction to the next level through persecution. How to move into a new location was a lesson taught by the Holy Spirit. I was driven by great opposition.

At the Headquarters Church Harvest Service held on 28th August 1994, the Spirit of God instructed me to present myself before the Church Elders and inform them of my decision to leave the Church as instructed by the Holy Spirit. This instruction was a bit difficult for me to adhere to, because I had intentionally bought my residential property very close to the church in order to have more devotional time. Also, I did not know where next to worship. But then, believing in the

Spirit within me, I waited until the end of the service before approaching the Leader and Minister-in-Charge, Senior Apostle Odufona. He is naturally a gentle and meticulous person, but my request to leave the Church shook him a bit. He asked me to wait for some time whilst he consulted with the remaining Elders. Their deliberation took a while, but eventually I was summoned.

The Church Leader thanked me for being honest, as many spiritualists had left the Church to establish their own places of worship without notifying the Headquarters. The Church Elders now asked if I would like the Headquarters to establish an arm of the Church for me, where I would be the Spiritualist in Charge. This I refused outright, as I was not so instructed spiritually. They then asked me what I expected the Headquarters to do for me. My answer was for all the Church Elders to pray for me that God would continue to lead me and be sovereign over my situation, repaying me for the services I rendered amongst them. They were very surprised at my response, but respectfully granted my request. The Church Elders at the Headquarters were very sympathetic towards me. I knelt in their midst and they prayed for me and released me with their blessings. Did God have a plan for my future? Yes, He did. I realised and recognised the significance of the Holy Spirit.

My departure from the C & S Headquarters in Earlham Grove Road had complications and struggles attached, yet knowing and trusting the power within me, I went ahead. My strength is in my struggle. For three months, daily prayers were held in the house with my children and two friends, but in November 1994, exactly three months after leaving Earlham Grove, help came from a total stranger who joined us in house worship. He linked me with the Church Minister of First Baptist Church, Romford Road, Ilford. Connection matters; move with those who believe in your destiny, because everything connected to you must say what you are saying and see alike with you if you are to build your vision out to reality.

The First Baptist Church Minister wanted to know the circumstances surrounding my leaving Earlham Grove, but I boldly told him that circumstances and flimsy excuses do not matter when Spiritual Call is in your life. My response kept him quiet. There and then I realised the Hand of the Lord is on me. We saw the birth of Holy Trinity Family Chapel (UK). If favour is in your life, you will always rise above obstacles. A lioness can be caged, but no one can stop it from roaring.

My mind-blowing God uses my little gifts despite my limitations and setbacks. What I was breaking into did not look like what I was breaking away from. This was a new spiritual rebirth. God got me ready for somewhere better than where I was. Life is a series of breakthrough. You must have the courage to see what is in the new dimension.

Chapter 12

ABUNDANT BLESSINGS

The first naming ceremony at Holy Trinity Family Chapel (UK) was of the Oladeji twins in 1996. Their mother joined us in worship prayers one evening dressed as a young spinster. Appearance can be deceptive. As she entered, the Spirit of God opened my eyes to see a vision of her surrounded by children. It was revealed that she would bear many children. The Spirit of the Lord strikingly told me that this woman would soon give birth to a set of twins, a boy and a girl,

Captain Mother Hasson at a Harvest Service in 1996

and God would take care of her. I made the revelation known to her, but to my dismay she told me that her main purpose in attending the prayer session was to pray for a good job and not for childbearing. She left the service disgruntled. About three months later, this lady joined the Church in prayers and again the same vision was relayed, even more clearly than before.

However, she did not leave in a hurry as she had before. No, she waited till the end of prayers, and there was a tall, strongly-built middle-aged man beside her, holding a baby in his hands. The man introduced himself as Mr Oladeji, and he did not mince his words, telling me off for my vision of his wife having many children. He said his wife came for prayers for gainful employment, but since my spiritual revelations they had found out that his wife was pregnant. Their young family was already blessed with four children, the youngest just four months old. I was left speechless. Tactfully, I explained the blessings attached to the vision and said that God's care was at hand.

After much persuasion, the man eventually agreed for the whole family to join the Church in worship. At the pre-natal appointment, the woman was confirmed pregnant with a set of twins. On delivery day, a phone call at dawn woke me up in summon to Newham General Hospital. The twins were delivered very early in the morning and the description matched the spiritual vision – a bouncing baby boy and a beautiful girl.

Mother Olu Hasson holding the Oladeji twins at a Thanksgiving Service in 1996

Mr Oladeji eventually served as our Church Secretary whilst his wife became a Welfare Officer. Their family's grandfather came from Nigeria and worshipped with us in Thanksgiving Service to God. If you have to tell people that you are a spiritualist, then you are not. Your works should speak for you.

At a Sunday church service in 1997, a pretty black ebony girl worshipped with us. After service she came to me and introduced herself as Gladys. She had driven from outside London to worship. Apparently her godmother had advised her to join our Church because she had a lot on her mind and wanted a breakthrough. I encouraged her to regularly attend the Friday protection and victory service. She agreed.

At her first protection and victory service, Gladys brought a pack of six bottles of water, each bottle representing a separate problem. She continued regularly bringing these bottles for a long time. Then came the time when Gladys ceased coming to Church. We were all worried, because it was unlike her to be absent. Then suddenly she resurfaced, beaming with smiles. She told me that the Lord Jesus Christ had heard her prayers in every way. She had met a handsome young man and fallen madly in love with him. In fact she was already expecting a baby.

She brought her man on a home visit to me, and their marriage was blessed at the Catholic Church with all our church members in attendance. The more you worship God, the more He blesses you with surprises.

Their baby girl arrived earlier than expected and had to be kept at the Royal Hospital for a period. Be confident in the time of trouble; pray until something happens. All we need is a little bit of faith to overcome all obstacles. We called on the Lord for miracle healing and He answered our prayers. We are endowed with the power to overcome struggles and troubles. The Spirit of the Lord named her Ebun Oluwa, meaning 'gift of God'. She is now an elegant lady.

Ours is a Holy Spirit-led chapel and as such when I was spiritually instructed in 1995 to sponsor our father in the Lord, Baba Aladura Samuel Abidoye, on a Holy Land pilgrimage, I complied immediately. I have learnt to listen to my instinct; the small soft voice always points me to my next move.

The Holy Spirit directed that the funds raised at the First Harvest of Holy Trinity Family Chapel (UK) must be utilised for this purpose. Fortunately for me, all the church members agreed with the spiritual instruction; there was no opposition. I had the cooperation of all. So, without wasting time, I contacted the Catholic-led Pilgrimage Organisers, St. Peter's Pilgrimages and paid the fares before informing Baba Abidoye himself.

In my childish and immature way, with exuberance and excitement, I hinted to a fellow church leader of the spiritual instruction and the steps I had so far taken. He was thrilled, and briefed a colleague of my spiritual mission; they both made a contribution towards the basic pocket money.

For spiritual maturity, one must resist and challenge childish ways. I have since learnt to outgrow the old ways of interactions, childish thoughts and responses, because I then started working on my immaturity. I have no choice but to grow up and move forward. You will only finish well if you focus on the tasks God has given you.

The Elder Stateman performed a successful holy pilgrimage to Israel in October 1995 and returned to a rousing welcome at the Heathrow Airport. At his Thanksgiving Service held at C & S Headquarters, Earlham Grove, London, Baba Aladura Abidoye told the congregation that he had arrived in Jerusalem exactly thirty years after the inauguration of Cherubim & Seraphim in Europe. He said that the reality of this fact stunned him. God's purpose is not always visible. Who could have predicted that he would worship in Jerusalem exactly 30 years after the Cherubim & Seraphim inauguration service in London? This could only be God's own doing. Baba Aladura Abidoye reaped the treasures of grace. I thank God for blessing him with age and authority. Everything God does is unique and different. Praise and thanks to the Almighty God.

I appreciate the position God placed me in then and the part He asked me to play. Looking at it now, everything I am going to be in the vineyard of God already exists in me. With patience, if I keep doing what He tells me, then He will open doors of favours and accomplishments in my life.

On the 26th May 2003, our Cherubim & Seraphim Overseas Headquarters suffered a terrible fire. In life, miracles and mysteries are related. You cannot have one without the other. What we can do is to pray that our miracles outlast our mysteries. I received the telephone call very early in the morning and was one of the first on the scene. What a calamity! The sight was devastating. Standing outside the premises, still in my pyjamas reminded me of the strong relationship I have with the Church. My spiritual root is there. Whether we confess it or not, all true believers are related to one another and we understand each other's circumstances. The 'see-saw of life' goes up and down. I saw the burden ahead of the congregation and reminded myself that to whom much is given, much is required. If you really want to enjoy the blessings of the Lord, pray for God to use you in sharing with those in need. If you deny the needy, then your blessing will become a burden, a holy thing in a filthy place. I did not wait for a word from God before making up my mind. I knew what to do. All the altar thrones, chairs and vestries at Holy Trinity Family Chapel (UK) were taken to our headquarters. I wanted to give more and more, to give all and everything, because this Church is my Root where I can relate.

Senior Mother Reverend Prophetess Hasson
Family Chapel Church
Sprowton Mews
Forest Gate

Dear Mother in Christ,

Re: Fire Damage Church Donation

We greet you in the name of our Lord Jesus Christ. The Spiritual Leader, Elders both male and female and the whole congregation express their gratitude and thanks to the beautiful chairs, alter table cloth and money you donated to the above your church. We take this opportunity to thank you for the love and devotion you have always shown towards this church especially on the day of the Fire Damage 26 May 2003.

We also thank you for assisting us in finding a solicitor for the church.

Our prayer is that the Almighty God will continue to Bless you, your family and your church will grow from strength to strength in Jesus name we pray. Amen

Yours in Christ,

Snr L/L Mary Babarinde
(General Secretary)

The Church is a member of the Council of Churches for Britain & Ireland, Churches Together in England and Cherubim & Seraphim Council of Churches (U.K)
REGISTERED AS CHARITY NO. 260353
(ALL CORRESPONDENCE TO THE GENERAL SECRETARY AT THE ABOVE ADDRESS)

Letter of appreciation from C & S Headquarters

Chapter 13

ECLIPSES AND CONFLICTS

Our Church, Holy Trinity Family Chapel (UK), is an African Pentecostal Church believing very much in spiritual messages and revelations. Regular revival services are encouraged and conducted. I invited a colleague, Prophetess Billingun, for a spiritual awakening revival, and she came along with an entourage. However, I noticed that a young man, Iye, who accompanied her on the revival, stayed behind, and called him in for an interrogation. He told me that he was following his spiritual instinct. Before long, he brought his pregnant wife, Kid, and two male accomplices. On seeing them, even while still far away, I could smell trouble in the air. Contacting my spiritual colleague, I pleaded with her to please recall his spiritual ward. Politely, she waved my pleadings aside, asking me not to worry over the 'stray' and saying that may be as he claimed, Iye had been spiritually guided to me.

Prophetess Billingun has a tendency to be clever. She is gifted and anointed, neither stupid nor careless. Deciding to show maturity and stability within the Church, and my own responsibility and decisiveness, I dropped the argument.

There was rapid growth in the Church congregation and spiritual development. Many young folks joined us in service. Also, Iye brought his friends in from another church, leaving the vulnerable elderly woman leader shattered. The newcomers and their leader, Iye, engaged in a blame game, blaming the elderly woman. They told me that a street runs both ways and that I should not pity the old woman. They could not seduce me with their praise singing. Do not be excited about those who praise you. However we treat people, Christ takes it personally.

Regular Bible study sessions were held for both young and old in the Church. Spiritualists were encouraged to study the holy book and the Church Pastor was sponsored for a Certificate in Religious

Studies course. On many occasions, I had to remind them that the Holy Spirit will not bring back to their heads what they have not kept there. In life, you have to master anything before you know it and learn because you have the opportunity. There is a difference between knowledge and wisdom. Knowledge can teach you how to operate a system, but Wisdom will teach you when to use it. The combination of both is perfection.

In all this development, Iye could not fit into the Church system. He presented himself as a teacher, when in actual fact he was still a suckling baby; not even weaned. He claimed to be the heir to the spiritual heritage. Iye needed to go through transition, but he was not willing.

My generosity was recognised and respected by Iye and his family, but there was more to him than met the eye. He was a chronic liar and womaniser. He was secretly sharing women among his inner circle of friends, passing the ladies from one to another. Fornicators are filthy people.

There are times in our lives when God puts us in situations where we cannot see. We cannot see the trees because we are busy cutting down the forest. By the time I realised what was going on, sex and stupidity were the order of the day. It is like running the Church with people who are dysfunctional.

Then Iye's pregnant wife delivered a baby boy. It was on the naming ceremony day that I knew the child had been born into a battle. Iye secretly invited an outsider to conduct the naming ceremony. Unfortunately for him, the invited guest was a direct descendant of my spiritual mentor, the greatest spiritual woman ever to live in my own race, the one and only replica of Holy Mary of our time, Abiodun Emmanuel. The true foundation of African Spiritualism was laid by the likes of her. So when a nutter planned a mockery, I knew I had to make a sacrifice in order to shame the devil. Hallelujah! The enemy's show did not slow me down, but he was left with the consequences of his stupidity. He was not only the joker but the joke. Iye uniquely and completely lost everything. The ceremony turned out to be a meeting of minds. I was flattered and extremely grateful.

Iye was flushed out with all his accomplices. I cannot stand a loser, especially a bad one. He hibernated in another neighbouring church, spreading his spiritual virus and false spiritual teachings, making a complete idiot of himself before his complete eradication. I am not a grudge holder but a grace receiver.

Do you know that conquering comes with conflicts? A young, vulnerable man, Demeji, was introduced to the Church by a lady prayerist, Alof, who claimed to be his sister. He requested prayer services and assistance. The Lord directed that he should have seaside prayers and I volunteered to go with him.

For the sake of fellow spiritualists reading this book, I would advise that it is better to draw a line between priesthood and parenthood. It is all about God's work; do it in God's way in order to be victorious. Be careful not to drag relationship and tradition into ministerial work. Our spiritual duties are sensitive. Sometimes what is around you is more dangerous than what is after you. Whatever it takes, go to God, let Him lead and follow His instructions.

At the seaside, we worshipped and praised God, clapping and dancing. We sought the Lord in prayers, narrating all the problems that pushed us out of our dwellings, bringing us to the seaside to seek God. If you really want something from God, you will walk, run and go out of your way to seek Him.

We do not deserve it, but God is Merciful. After all's said and done, put yourself in a position to receive His mercy. When He answers our prayers, we dance before Him.

Some pressmen from the local Echo newspaper were attracted by our mode of worship and they recorded everything, after which they approached us for questioning. To satisfy their curiosity, I answered all their questions and explained the spiritual aspect of our mission. At this point, Demeji became afraid. He pulled me aside to confide that he was an illegal immigrant in the country and any publication could lead to Immigration arrest. I gave him the assurance that it would never come to that and asked him to be brave. My words calmed him down a little. I do not blame him; we cannot be brave without first feeling fear.

They asked for permission for publication in the newspaper and the following day, Tuesday September 3 2002, our photo was published.

Captain Mother Hasson holding a seaside service with Demeji

In life, everybody has a devil messenger; it could be anger, poverty or sickness. However in Demeji's case it was his sister, Alof, the one who had introduced him to the Church. He thought that because they were from the same tribe and she was much older than him, the woman was only helping him in his time of need. You can give the devil a run if you have not been dating him. Do not swap bondage.

Sometimes situations change, but in Demeji's case, they stayed the same because Alof brought baggage into his new life. She became aggressive, manipulative and poisonous. But because he depended on her for economic and emotional support, the woman got all she wanted. Alof is a specialist in how to take advantage of the moment. My intervention was vehemently rebuked.

The image she presented to me was contradictory to the reality. This prayerist woman, Alof, told me bluntly that she was going to marry Demeji whether I liked it or not; that God should pave a way for the marriage despite all the discrepancies attached. There are situations that sometimes knock you to your knees. This was one of them. How do you win the fight if the enemy is your closest ally?

Alof shouted at me angrily, "Why are you not like other people, other spiritualists? Why are you always different? Other Spiritualists will support me," she added, before storming out of the church.

It is a dangerous thing to be like other people; learn to be yourself. Never be ashamed of who you are. Develop, appreciate and celebrate your uniqueness.

Because of my objection, she uprooted Demeji and took him to another Church and introduced him as her husband. As for me, she went around spreading rumours and gossips about me not wishing anyone happiness and promised to deal with me in many ways from various angles. This is a case of "I have an enemy and the enemy is my friend". Alof was not boasting;

she tried everything in her power to hurt, maim and even kill, but all her efforts failed.

Let nobody ask me Alof's whereabouts today, for she is where she placed herself yesterday. As you lay your bed, so shall you sleep on it. I am in the wheel of God and still fighting for survival. But as God is on my side, I will win every battle.

I see myself as one of the old breed and my background reflects on most of what I say and think. This is a good attribute, but it exposes me to furious attacks as many enemies could read me like a book. I have many times passed through terrible situations, but my Lord and God has been with me, thereby making the best of impossible and bad situations.

Chapter 14

FINANCIAL BOOM AND DOOM

In life, God's expectation is for us to be great, so it is essential that you maximise your opportunities without fear and develop the instinct to increase and win. You never have an increase if you are controlled by fear. If you do not want any trouble, you do not want any increase. Plan ahead and have foresight. The best way to live in life is to see past your present day.

If we handle our new opportunities well, we are definitely ready for higher level. Instinct is the power to push at the right moment; it tells us when to do things, but we must find access to our new dimension. We are exposed to the same information, but processing differs; it affects outcome. One needs to be strong and courageous.

I followed my instinct in the early 90s and ventured into freehold properties, knowing full well that I was running a race for the future of my young family. At a time, there were four high standard properties in my portfolio. All was not smooth sailing, but my financial talents were well used. The global economic crisis and deep recession recently suffered by the real estate market exposed my family to greater risks and financial loss. We went into operation with profitability without the risk incurred in mind.

How would you feel if you lost three properties in a single day? For that was what happened. In one day, I placed three properties, including my own home, residence and palace, on the market for sale.

The truth, of course, is that signs of financial chaos were erupting all around us. Property prices were plunging daily. Businesses noticed that fewer people were coming in and those that did had less money to spend. Economic activity slowed down. In fact, the world was facing a financial crisis. Of course nobody can forget what happened. We had problems with tenants and law suits and cases were looming. News about economic slowdown was in the headlines almost every single day. It was not going to get better any time soon.

I took up jobs for meagre wages; I even worked in hospitals doing clinical administration. I went through dry places, tiredness, exhaustion of pleasure, loss of joy and lack of smiles. When I could not take it anymore, I travelled to Israel to seek God, because by then I was on the verge of committing suicide. I was stressed, emotionally homeless and spiritually helpless.

While I was there, the Lord placed a song on my mind, the content of which was the answer to my financial crisis. Through it all I learned to trust in God.

Within months, the crisis was resolved. I moved house, changed work and boycotted everything that could be boycotted. It was not easy, but it was worthwhile. I retired earlier than my colleagues and I am enjoying every minute of it. God saved me, in spite of all my weaknesses.

I still see this aspect of my life as unfinished business. I may dabble in properties again if there is a relevant purpose for me to fulfil. Hopefully the success therein will still keep me in the presence of my God.

Chapter 15

WALKING IN A MINEFIELD

An elderly Christian leader, Pa Kofi Austin, whom I met whilst worshipping at the C & S Church, Earlham Grove, East London, summoned me to his house in April 2006. He was an old man and had disabilities which made him housebound. With the type of background I have, when an Elder calls, you respectfully respond without question. Never be afraid to be humble, because you will be exalted.

At his flat in Stratford, East London, we had a

heart-to-heart talk during which he explained that our meeting was fated and our shared jokes and belief made us bond. Therefore, not only did he want me to be his confidant, he wanted to entrust me with his savings. He explained that he had entrusted a friend with his money but that he had embezzled it.

Pa Austin's requests shocked me and made me very uncomfortable. He placed me on a very sensitive threshold which needed great common sense, sensibility and discipline. My first reaction was to humbly turn down his requests, for personal reasons. He was elderly, weak and blind. Also, he had his relations living with him and any one of them could have fitted into the position he was placing me. Most of all, I saw his requests as dragging me back to where I was running away from. To live in the present began in the past.

Questions started racing in my mind. How would I handle somebody else's money? Would I use my position to be selfish? Is this a trying test for me? How would I differentiate between love and lust, self-serving creed? My inner self told me that I was being tested between love and lust; my faith and background were on test. Whatever reason there was for this situation in which I found myself, I knew that I must pass this test because I was being validated. Nothing prepared me for handling and overcoming the test of lust and greed. I had to dig down to my background and foundation for support. The test came to try me. I must settle for love over lust and selfishness, because lust takes but love gives.

Pa Austin was very persuasive. He told me not to say "No" when God says "Go". He convinced me that God had sent me to help him; your ability is being watched before you get the opportunity.

Lifting up his pillow, he handed me an envelope containing the sum of two hundred and fifty pounds. That was the start of the savings. From time to time he would call requesting a visit from me, or send me envelopes in order to add to his savings. This was the pattern over a long period.

Although he was a bit strict and set in his ways, I found Pa Austin vibrantly brilliant, always talking in riddles, jovial and very light at heart. He was funny, thoughtful and uplifting. Eventually my conclusion was that he trusted me, but I needed to earn his respect as well.

This arrangement put me at an advantage, but Pa Austin was at my mercy. What would I do? How would I behave? I had to confide in someone. I made the arrangement between Pa Austin and myself known to both my Church Secretary and Church Pastor, who sometimes escorted me on visits to this elderly man. Also, as an act of charity, I arranged regular home visits with hampers of foods and drinks. A church member, Sarah Dayo, who lived nearby to him, was always happy and eager to deliver food and drinks baskets.

At Christmas time, every year, I personally delivered the accrued interest on his savings to Pa Austin. He gave this out to his immediate family members as Christmas gifts. It was odd that none of his own children was ever seen around. However, his cousins, nephews and friends became his extended family members and really took great care of him. Pa Austin was greatly loved and cared for by those around him. They devoted time and energy to look after him. He was a lucky man and highly favoured at his old age to receive such excellent care.

In June 2012, exactly six years after the inauguration of our savings arrangement, the Lord showed me a hint of what was to happen. In my dream, I found myself dressed in full ministerial regalia walking along the neighbourhood at sunset. On my left-hand side was a gathering of friends, drinking and in relaxing mood. Pa Austin was among them. The senior most amongst them called my name; pointing to Pa Austin, he said "This friend of ours, Kofi Austin, told us in this club that while he was alive, you looked after him. He entrusted you with his money and you never embezzled it. We all noticed your generosity to him. Thank you for looking after him. He is now with us and we brought you here to give you a fitting reward for your honesty." He paused. Continuing, he prayed, "You will not work for money; money will work for you. Your life challenges will make you become a great champion."

Lifting the goblet from the table, he prayed and blessed me immensely. He then passed the goblet to the next person to him and he prayed likewise. So did all of them; they were six elderly men in a circle. I stood still while they were pouring thoroughly engrossing prayers over me. Then I woke up.

I did not need anyone to interpret the dream. Its meaning was glaringly clear. Though Pa Austin was still alive and kicking, he was spiritually gone; already he was with his friends in the celestial realm. Things start in the spiritual realm before the physical realm. Survival in the spiritual zone is seeing and yet not being seen.

That same day, I made a casual visit Pa Austin. At the end of our conversation, I asked him to please invite his cousin for an arranged meeting, as there was a message for her. He arranged a meeting for us in his flat on the 8th December 2012 at 7pm. There were four of us present at the meeting, including Madam Audrey, Pa Austin's friend.

Thanking him for his trust and confidence in me, I reminded him of our first meeting and his request of me. I asked him if he knew how much was in his savings account, to which he replied £15,000 (fifteen thousand pounds). I corrected him; his money was now up to £16,135 with interest added. Lifting myself up from the chair, I moved closer to him on his bed and put a bank certified cheque in his hands. I informed him that the Lord had specifically told me to return his money.

The whole atmosphere was quiet. Nobody saw that coming; it was a great surprise. None of them knew that Pa Austin had such a large amount of money in his savings. He had started with £250 and it grown up to £16,135 over a period of six years.

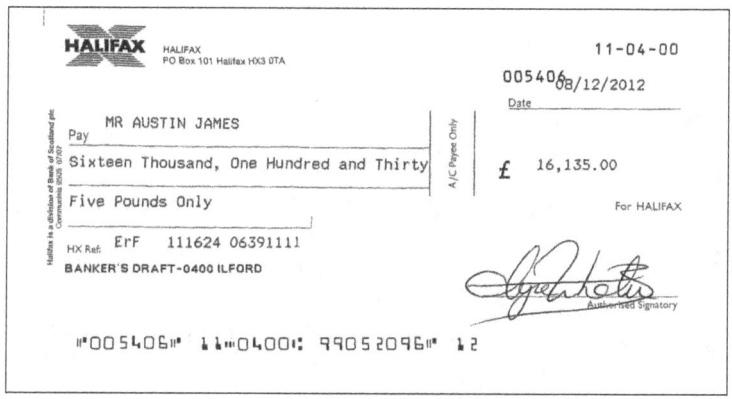

Bank certified cheque issued for Pa Kofi Austin

Pa Austin died on died January 26 2014. The revelation was not too long ago. My consolation was that he lived well and was well looked after. He died peacefully surrounded by those who loved him.

Some days after he had passed away, an elderly community woman called me and from her salutations was bidding me to ensure that Pa Austin received a befitting burial, as I was the sole custodian of his money and assets. She told me that from the grapevine, the whole community was waiting to hear the great burial plan being arranged by me. All eyes were on me. Has any problem kept you awake all night? Yes, this kept me staring at the ceiling all night, secretly praying for divine intervention on this matter. Overnight, the spirit within advised me to deal with the root of the issue before dealing with the fruits. I was spiritually instructed to visit the Elders at the Cherubim & Seraphim Headquarters, briefing them of the transactions between Pa Austin and myself and letting them know the true situation of things, as I had nothing to hide. I had to save my reputation, my position and my background.

As humility is always the way to exaltation, the following day, with humility, I requested a meeting with the Church Elders. The quickest way to go up is to go down first; whatever it takes, humility first.

On the last Sunday in February 2014, a meeting was convened with the Elders and I attended with my Church Secretary, Evangelist Adeoye and a community chief. There were ten Elders in attendance. It was a full house. I narrated all transactions and presented copies of documents to them. Most of the Elders were already aware of the grapevine rumours, but a few were unaware. My enemies were ruling without glory. Whilst still presenting my case and documents, some Elders were on their feet asking God for forgiveness for capitalising on rumours and jumping to conclusions.

The meeting lasted for one and half hours. I am

very grateful to God for His divine inspiration and intervention. I felt healed, as He solved the problem superficially.

My enemies went crazy with envy and jealousy, because they did not have the grace of God, which I have and enjoy every day. There are people who are offended by you doing well; they are limited people. Their little voices were silenced. I do not know why people were intimidated by me.

I cried unto the Lord in prayer, "Arise O Lord and let your enemies be scattered". Christ stood up for me. I know that God is for me. Even when life turns against me, God is with me. I felt used, stabbed in the back and lied about by ungrateful and unappreciative people, but I did not reciprocate. I allowed myself to be abused by some idiots so that I could do what I was called to do.

My enemies owe my God a big "thank you" because He asked me to be nice to them and not to take them to court. I wanted to sue these slanderers for defamation of character. This whole episode has taught me a lesson. When you throw yourself into an assignment unselfishly, then God is working on your own problem. I was on the verge of a reward. God turned their victimisation around to victory and favour for me.

To my admirers and antagonists, I am the best of the best; every element of wonder. I endured, accomplished and prevailed through the power of God in me. The power behind me is greater than the tasks ahead of me. The testing is over. After this ordeal, exceeding blessings started rolling in. I passed! My enemies can go to hell for me, as I do not have to.

Chapter 16

BEYOND BELIEF ENCOUNTERS

The world is so perverse that understanding it is almost impossible for human minds. It is a world beyond belief. One must develop outwardly and inwardly to understand one's immediate surroundings. However, there is another side of this worldly arena that is not commonly known by all, as its revelation is only to a chosen handful. I am talking about the unseen spiritual world surrounding us. In it, all things are firstly made to be, only to become materialistic and realistic in the physical world later.

In the spiritual realm, mortal mind has no control. Everything has been ordained by the Supreme Being and unseen forces. There is no room for immaturity or failure. There, the past and the future are rolled together to determine the present. It takes the deep to hear the deep.

Despite the fact that I have had the opportunities of making so many spiritual journeys in my lifetime, I still find it difficult to describe the revelations. I have moved from familiar states into unfamiliar positions and the purposes of my journeys have been distinctively similar – the revelation and confirmation of another world. The strength of our life purpose and destiny is not hindered or controlled by our environment but preordained by the Supreme power in the Spiritual realm. His presence is in every process. Time and purpose is in God's hands and when He combines the two together in your favour, you will be brought from the background to the front line at the right time.

I would like to share with you my spiritual journey experiences, and some hard to interpret dreams.

1. In September 1973, I was living in Calabar, the capital of South Eastern Nigeria. I had a very good job as a stenographer to the Commissioner of Police. Life was comfortable.

Whilst having a siesta one day, I had a dream. A young man in the robes of priesthood discussed my

Christian faith with me. He asked me many questions which I correctly answered. At the end of a prolonged dialogue, he told me that I would have to choose between Catholicism and spiritualism, as the two cannot be practised together. Moreover, whatever choice I made, there would be no chance of reverting back. No going back, no change of mind.

After deep thought, I made my choice – spiritualism. He accepted my choice and told me that God would gradually, step-by-step, bring me into revelations; that I should wait on Him. He instantly departed. I woke up and realised it had been a dream. Our dreams and visions disclose future events and prepare us for the future.

2. Almost a month after this, in October 1973 to be precise, I had a spiritual ordeal. Orchestrated music woke me up from sleep and kept me awake for hours on my bed. It was deafening, but it was also a perfectly pitched masterpiece, beautiful and endearing. I rushed out to draw the attention of the night watchmen to the deafening music. They politely told me that there was no music or noise in the area. Apparently I was the only one hearing it. Quietly I returned to bed, where I fell into a deep sleep and began to dream.

The entire sky turned dark; darkness covered everywhere from the sky to the sea. Looking up, I saw a small shining star descending. However, as it descended towards me, it was changing shape into various things. Firstly, the star changed into a ship; still descending, it changed to a large aeroplane, followed by a flat flying saucer. Eventually, on landing, it changed into a dwarf. He was smartly dressed and in his hand was a tiny trumpet. He blew his trumpet, with a loud tone, into the four corners of the world with a message "Be of good deeds, so that the same can be recorded for you". Four times he blew his trumpet and four times the same message echoed throughout the whole world.

His departure was of the same style as his arrival. He changed into all the former modes, flew up into the dark sky and disappeared. I stood still, my neck stretched as far as I could and my jaw dropping. I woke up with the message ringing in my ears. I felt light and graceful flowing in God's spirit.

3. In April 1974, I left my post in Calabar only to relocate at Ile-Ife, the cradle city of the Yorubas. Initially I did not welcome the change, but the crisis which ensued was a set up for the Glory of God in my life. I had found myself in a bad marriage. My family isolated me because I did not heed their warnings and advice. Publicly, I was humiliated and embarrassed because my partner was committing atrocities. He was power drunk. Through it all, I held on to my faith and glued to God.

One day, after a night vigil service, I had a dream. In it, there was a spiral staircase in a large building and I was asked to climb it to the top. On top of the staircase there were about twenty Elders, robed in immaculate white garments. High top hats adorned their white flaky hair as they gracefully sat around a conference table awaiting my arrival. I was invited in.

They Elders were black men and women, very old. They looked the same but were not the same. They were all champions in their own individual right.

On entry, they welcomed me and introduced themselves. Looking around, I could recognise only two of them; Baba Moses Orimolade and Captain Abiodun Emmanuel. I had never met any of them in real life. The Elders told me that all of them had been on spiritual missionary duties to various parts of the world but at different times, dating back as far as eight hundred years. Their spokesman told me that they had brought me up to send me on an errand because much was required of me. He advised that I must not be intimidated by critics, as many would rise up against me. Instead, I should stand for the truth; be honest and kind. He said that the Spirit within me would take me to far away nations. Finally, he instructed me to have courage to act on whatever I saw in spirit. Then they blessed and released me back to my own time.

On waking up, I knew there and then that there was a great purpose for my life and belief. God had lit a fire in my heart to seek and serve Him.

4. A Belief in the Afterlife

The year 1977 was a great one for the African continent. The festival of Arts and Culture was on, bringing all blacks back home. I thought it was for the living only. How wrong I was.

One Saturday in August, my room was suddenly filled with fresh breeze and I fell into a deep sleep. There standing before me was my dead mother. She looked terribly upset and worried. Coming closer to me, she instructed me to quickly visit a relation and warn him of the consequence of the visitors he was harbouring in his house. What an ordeal! Bluntly I refused, because the person concerned was a very strict man and never welcomed any intruding busybodies in his life. Moreover, the gap in our life styles, age and affluence was so huge that going to deliver such a message would be regarded as an insult to him.

All these reasons I made known to my mother, but they all fell on deaf or dead ears. I could see that she was worried; she was fidgeting and pacing up and down the room. After a brief moment she told me that our relation sought help from some mason members who had given him some charms for protection. Unknown to him, the charms lived by sucking human blood. In addition to this havoc, the charms would ward off any evil encounter in the family, but then nothing good would come into the household. You could not have one without the other, but the evils outweighed the goodness received. She begged me to please help her because the evil charms prevented her from entering his house.

Moved with pity for her and concern for my relation, I agreed to comply with her request. Immediately after my consent, I woke up. What a dream!

I wasted no time in digesting the instruction given. Quickly I rushed out on the errand. It took me a long time to reach my relation's house. The children and their mothers were in, but he was not. He had been away since dawn attending a meeting in Ibadan; he was not expected back until the following day. His wives could read the seriousness of my visit and tried to persuade me to leave a message. I could not do that. The message was strictly private and too delicate to relay. So I left the house.

I was just about to cross the road when my relation's car drove past. He did not see me. Retracing my steps, I ran back to his house, trying to get into the compound before him. I got there just about at the same time the gateman was opening the garage.

My relative was surprised to see me running up almost out of breath. Waving my hand, I told him of the afternoon visit and the ensuing dialogue with mother. He was quiet and stood still throughout my explanations. It was as if he had lost his voice. When he eventually spoke, his utterance nearly made me faint. He said that all that Mama had said was true and that the charms were his personal bodyguards. Also, he confirmed that his friends, who were members of a local masons' club, had introduced the charms for security, protection and promotion at work. Asking him if he knew the charms were feeding on human blood, he replied negatively.

When he eventually found his voice, he asked me why my dead mother had not come to him directly. "Why did she send you?" he questioned. My reply was not far-fetched. It was because the charms prevented her from coming in; they debarred her entry. By sending me to deliver this message, she was exposing me to the truth. A mother's love is more powerful than anything.

When I left his house, he was still standing by his car, dazed and confused. Who says the dead are gone forever? No, they are very much around. This episode affirms my belief in the afterlife.

5. Grace Pleads for Mercy

My first spaceship journey was in 1985. In a dream, I saw a flying saucer descending and there in the mid-air, the side door opened. A uniformed flight attendant stepped out. He came straight to where I was and delivered a message that I was summoned. Looking around me, on the balcony of my house I saw a small side table with a glass and a bottle of Guinness stout.

Apparently, I was just having some relaxation. What a life!

However, immediately I heard the message, there was no urge to argue; I felt I had to follow him. We walked on air towards the parked spaceship. He pressed the control on his hand to open it and on entry, he locked the ship with the same remote control. The control, I later realised, had purposeful uses. He scanned me from head to toe. I asked him the reason for the scanning, and he politely explained that it was to disarm me of any earthly power and also to make me lighter in weight in readiness for the fast journey ahead. He escorted me to my seat and attached my seat belt. All he did was strange to me, but everything was to ensure my safety.

Looking around, I saw that the ship was manned by a pilot. The interior was very bright, immaculate, white and cool. My seat was soft and very comfortable. The structure within was the same as outside, round and flat. Prior to this journey, I had never entered a plane before. The spaceship travelled extremely fast. We seemed to be covering a thousand miles in a flash. At that particular moment, there was nothing I could do but to submit to fate. God sometimes expects something from us which we are not used to giving. In my own case, it is submission.

At long last, the spaceship landed on a large field of pure white salt. The land was endless and everywhere was pure snowy white. There was no earthly soil, only salt. The only structure was a giant snow-white rocket tower, hundreds of metres in height. The pilot escorted me inside the building.

On observation, the interior had seven floor levels. On the ground floor was a nursery of uncountable human babies, yet unborn, waiting for earthly deliveries. The first floor harboured the dead people of all nations. They were alive in their own bodily forms, so I could distinguish one nationality from another. Passing through, one of them drew me close to himself, but was warned by my Pilot to lay his hands off me because I was summoned and yet to report. At last we entered a reception area, a large room with one table and a chair. Sitting on the chair was a receptionist, a blind lady. She had her head bent down towards the table as if she was reading, but she was not. There was nothing on the table.

As we entered, I saw stacked in a corner my chair, my small side table, my glass and my bottle of Guinness. An unseen force pushed me towards the Guinness and I found myself sitting on my earthly chair. Immediately I felt as if my body had been plugged into an electric socket. My right arm was as red as hot iron. I was electrified and in serious pains. I was on fire, inside the furnace of hell; roasting and roaring.

The pilot announced our arrival. He called the receptionist by her name, Grace. He then told her that he had just brought me back, as instructed, from

Nigeria, Africa. Grace now lifted her face up off the table. It was then I realised that she was blind. Her eyelids were closed and she had to lift them up with her fingers in order to have a look at me.

Adjacent to the reception was a room. There came a loud voice of notification from there saying that a bottle of life fluid had just been lowered into the room and that the life it represented was in serious agony. On hearing this announcement, Grace leapt up, pleading that the soul it represented was with her at the reception but in great pain. She pleaded for mercy. The voice now granted her request, allowing me inside the room.

There were four men walking around in the room, all wearing white robes. I could only see the edges of their robes and their feet. Right in the centre of the room was the bottle of life fluid. The men raised their voices up in prayer, asking God to please remove the burning pain. Swiftly the electric current was switched off and the pain subsided a little. I was still screaming but at the same time, I was relieved enough to answer their questions.

On the ground beside me was a bottle and a small card. The card was filled with graphic lines, all representing areas of my life. To an onlooker, it was just an ordinary paper. However, in the hands of the men the paper contained an analysis of my entire life. The paper contained relevant information about me - my name, date and place of birth, my parents' names and other information. Every minute of my life was accounted for by graphic strokes on the paper.

When my name was read out, there was complete silence and disappointment in the room. Their leader bent down, looking at me as if to confirm who I was. He then told me that I was a Captain Mother and Queen, in the spiritual realm. I had been sent on an earthly mission but was now returning unfulfilled and unaccomplished, I could never be accepted back into my position. He told me that all my maids were waiting for me, but it would break their hearts to see me as I was. My return should be marked with great celebrations befitting my position.

The four Elders and Grace, the receptionist, wept for me. They raised their voices up for mercy and asked that I be granted another chance to perform and measure up to expectation. After what looked like days of pleading, both the bottle and card were drawn up. They explained that I would be allowed to return to earth, but this time around I must ensure that I completed all the charitable and ministerial tasks assigned to me. I was given a second chance to live up to expectations.

Grace then gave me a lecture on expectations. She promised to be an empowering agent for me and to keep me covered. All the assignments God had given me to do, Grace would give me the knowledge and ability to accept and face all challenges. My promise to her was that I would accept responsibility for the second chance and gifts given to me. I would work towards releasing the Spirit inside and build on the Grace of God in my life. God's glory would come out and shine through me by His Grace. Grace pleaded for mercy.

Finally the pilot led me to the spaceship and brought me back to the very spot where he had picked me up from.

So I have a home somewhere in a wonderful, supernatural, celestial world beyond this earthly dwelling place. I know where I come from, and I am proud of that.

6. An Element of Wonder

My dream in June 1991 was what I call an element of wonder. A rocking, cracking noise disturbed my deep sleep and woke me up. I found myself in a coffin, fully dressed as a corpse, in white clothes. The coffin cracked and I stood up, looking for my children. I remembered calling out for my kids. Around, there were a great number of other dead fellows getting up and dusting themselves. There was no tree or structure, just a vast open space, miles and miles of endless space.

Then sweet, blissful music started filling the cool atmosphere with glorious praises of the Most High God. Every soul was calm, comfortable and at peace. We needed nothing but water. And if the urge arose, we would go to a water fountain which automatically emerged from underneath, levelling to your mouth and giving you a cool refreshing mouthful. There I enjoyed peace surpassing any earthly understanding.

7. Call to Spiritual Retreat

On a Monday morning in March 1994, I was on my way to work in Leyton, East London, at 8 am when suddenly I felt the Hand of the Lord on me. I was in spirit. Managing to get close to the bus stop shelter, I held on to the post and stood still for some time before returning home. That was the beginning of a three-day spiritual journey. The senior spiritualist at Cherubim & Seraphim Church, Earlham Grove London, Prophet Saibu, came to my house and took me to the Prayer House. He was with me throughout the period of my spiritual journey and he stood by me.

On the first day of my trance, I was endowed with a new gift, a beautiful Arabic book of verses and prayers. It was strange but wonderful, as I had never attended an Arabic school. I would pray in sweet Arabic tone for hours and recite the Bible verses without stopping. God is the only One who can give you a spiritual makeover.

On the second day, I asked the Spirit within me to reveal himself to me. I just wanted to know what was happening to me. There embedded in me was a piece of hard solid rock, highly inflamed, with a bright burning flame. I wish there were words to explain what I saw and how surprised I was. It was an embrace of spiritual intimacy; a period when the Holy Spirit met His own.

Throughout the period of my spiritual journey, my voice was as clear as crystal. No food, no drinks, but I was full of energy.

On the third day, my guiding spirit took me away to a strange land. There was no house there but a large open hall the size of a great city. The hall had only one entrance gate with a small side door. On reaching the gate, I knocked on the door and there was a response. Behind the slightly opened door was an elder asking me for the password with the question "Who do you believe in?" My answer was on my lips; "I believe in God through Jesus Christ". He raised his brow with a questioning look and asked me again: "Who is Jesus Christ?" This time the startled look was on my face. "So, you don't know Jesus Christ, the Saviour of the world?" In a very soft-spoken voice, my guardian spirit whispered into my ears that Jesus Christ is known in the realm as the Lamb of God. So I replied the elder at the door that I believe in God and serve Him through the Lamb of God. "Oh! Ah, you are welcome. You believe in the Lamb of God!"

On his proclamation of the Lamb of God, the whole assembly, uncountable in number, all in white dazzling robes, fell on their faces in reverence and praise of the Lamb. Their voices were so smooth, sweet and inviting. At once, he opened the side door for me to enter. In a flash, my guarding spirit snatched me away from the gate. He was so fast whisking me away that we were flying in the air at a high speed.

When we landed, my guarding spirit explained to me that I was just a fraction of a second from death. Explaining further, he said that many spiritualists in trance unexpectedly slip away into oblivion, either because their guarding spirits were not observant enough or the spiritualists could not resist joining the music and praise of the worship. He had taken me there to observe the way of worship and not to join them. The City of Praise harbours the souls of the departed Saints; they praise and worship God ceaselessly. There is neither day nor night there; time is endless. No living soul comes out once allowed in. Whoa! I had had a lucky escape.

8. Help the Dying in Need

At the Holy Trinity Family Chapel Harvest in September 1995, printed copies of the 1996 calendar were distributed to all members and invited guests. The calendar displayed the pictures and names of the Church Minister, Church Secretary, and all necessary information about the church address, telephone numbers and times of worship. All attendees were encouraged to take a copy home. An invited guest, Mrs Oshinowo, collected her own copy and displayed it on her wall at home.

One evening in July 1996, I received a telephone call from an anonymous caller. She informed me that that Mrs Oshinowo, who was her neighbour, was very sick at the hospital and that I should visit her. I was a bit hesitant at the request to visit her at the hospital. I told the caller that Mrs Oshinowo's name was not familiar to me as I did not know anyone bearing such a name. "If you do not know her, how come your church calendar is in her sitting room?" she queried. Reluctantly, I collected the hospital details from her, promising to visit soon.

The following day, my husband and I visited Mile End General Hospital, East London to see Mrs Oshinowo. On arrival at reception, the medical staff notified her doctor immediately and he called my husband aside to advise that his patient was severely sick and that family members should be notified. She had respiratory and heart problems. She was dying. Anyway, he led us to where the sick woman was.

There were drawn curtains around her bed. She had tubes on her chests and nostrils connecting to cylinders. We greeted each other and introduced ourselves, and she recognised me. For a brief period, we said some prayers. As we all could see that her health situation was really bad, I then asked for permission to administer the last Christian rite. We had not brought any wafers or wine, so I had to return home for all necessary items.

The last rite anointing and holy communion

administration was brief. The wafer was soaked in the wine and placed in between her teeth, while holy oil anointing was administered. Mrs Oshinowo realised all that was happening around her. She was constantly nodding her head in support.

Our names and contact numbers were left with her doctor and at the reception in case of any emergency. We left the hospital with heavy hearts, knowing that we might not be seeing her again.

After having no news for two whole days, we decided to check on our parishioner patient at the hospital during the evening visiting period. Surprisingly, Mrs Oshinowo was lying comfortably on her bed without any tubes or strings attached. On seeing us, she dragged herself up to a sitting position. We were shocked beyond words; we opened our mouths, but no sound came out. She smiled and beckoned us to sit beside her. What should we call this? She thanked God for her surprise rapid recovery. She told us that the medical staff were marvelling at her unexplained recovery. We were all happy for her.

As visiting time was over, I told her that I would be going on an Israel (Jerusalem) pilgrimage within the next week and my preparations would prevent me from making further visits. Since she was now getting better, I would visit her at home on my return from Israel. Immediately, she jumped out of her bed, saying that her doctor had already hinted that she would be fit for discharge at the weekend. She would be fit to travel with us to Israel!

Alas, the only hindrance was her financial status. She had no money, although she was expecting some payments at the end of the month. She begged and cried for my assistance. Do not be tough on people who are weak; if you want mercy, be merciful to others. We must be trusted to be generous; God gives to giving people. If God can give it through you then He will give it to you. I knew that I had something that God wanted to use, so I paid for Mrs Oshinowo's pilgrimage to the Holy Land. She was so happy.

In early August 1996, I was privileged to lead a group of Christian believers on an eight-day holy pilgrimage to Israel. We were 20 in number and Mrs Oshinowo was among us. The outward flight and landing were very smooth. There was great expectation and enthusiasm within the group. When we stepped outside the Tel Aviv Airport, some pilgrims kissed the ground and wept for joy.

The first four days were spent in Tiberias, Cana and Magdala, all in the southern part of Israel. Our itinerary was very comprehensive, full of activities, and everyone was willing and eager, ever ready to fulfil our Christian missionary commitment.

On the third day, our itinerary took us to the River Jordan baptismal site. As a Church Minister, I wore my richly embroidered robes. Following a church service, we had a wonderful water immersion for both old and new converts. Baptism and rededication is the nerve centre of our religious activities. The whole service was fun and exciting. At the end of the day, we all felt reborn, our sins and guilt washed away. No conviction but correction and connection to God without any condemnation.

When we gathered for morning prayers, Mrs Oshinowo told us that she had had a dream in the night. She had found herself back at the baptismal site, swimming in the river, so cool and relaxing. According to her account, she was so comfortable that she decided not to come out, so she drifted with the current peacefully. Although I knew what this meant, I refused to comment openly.

At midday, I took her aside for a heart-to-heart talk. She bravely told me that she understood the meaning of her dream and that I should not worry myself. But the only problem on her mind was a rift between her and her eldest daughter, who lived in America. She had not been on good terms with her for over ten years. She would like the rift settled. Mrs Oshinowo told me that her daughter was very stubborn and as custom demanded, her daughter should be the first person to apologise. Her response was childish, and that was why I was a bit hard on her. I just told her that the little child in her was still talking in her adult life. Immaturity was keeping her in a situation she should have overcome. Our old ways can sometimes be dysfunctional, and in her own case, it was blocking the progress of her relationship with her daughter. My advice to her was to buy a beautiful Bible from the Holy Land, engrave both her name and her daughter's name on it and send it to her in America. She was delighted with the advice but had no money. So I paid for the Bible.

On another day at the morning prayers, as usual, pilgrims stood up to share spiritual instructions and revelations. Mrs Oshinowo got up and told us that in her dream she had had a reunion with her late husband. Their marriage was blessed in a church and rings were exchanged between the two. All the pilgrims diverted their focus to me for interpretation but as before, I kept mute. In truth my mind was disturbed greatly, because all her dreams, though different, meant the same. I was leading a group of mature individuals and I was not going to let them miss the pilgrimage pleasures of a lifetime, so we all focused on our pilgrimage itinerary.

We flew back to London on Friday night to the delight of friends and family members who congratulated us on our spiritual voyage. What an outstanding spiritual accomplishment.

Two days later, we all attended the Church Thanksgiving Service. All pilgrims were present including Mrs Oshinowo. Immediately after the thanksgiving session, she called me aside to say that she had forgotten to take her prescription in the morning so she had gone to the kitchen to administer it whilst the service continued. On instinct, I popped in to see how she was. She asked me to call the ambulance for her. On arrival, the ambulance team came to the kitchen and escorted her away into the waiting vehicle. A church orderly went with her. When the orderly returned an hour later, he reported that Mrs Oshinowo had passed away in the ambulance. She was reported dead on arrival.

We managed to keep the news quiet at the service, but none of the officiating ministers believed it. This was a woman who had come out giving thanks and dancing before the crowd, only to be pronounced dead an hour later.

On getting home, I briefed my husband of the incident at the service and of Mrs Oshinowo's death. He was not surprised at all. He said that what really baffled him was the woman going on the pilgrimage. In his words, "that woman died a long time ago, even before she travelled with you on the pilgrimage". She was only given the grace to visit Israel on pilgrimage. She did not do any other thing after that. I learnt a great deal from this task.

A whole year passed before, at a Sunday service, a young girl came forward to present me with a bouquet of flowers during praise worship session. She introduced herself as the last child of Mrs Oshinowo and said her mother had confided in her before she travelled to the Holy Land that I had paid her fares and given her pocket money. On her return from Israel, she showed her the engraved Bible and asked her to send it to her elder sister in America. Her senior sister was at their mother's funeral because of the words inscribed on the Holy Book by her mother. The feud was settled.

On the anniversary of Mrs Oshinowo's death, the children decided to settle all her outstanding debts. The girl was at the service to give me a cheque for their mother's pilgrimage costs and a "Thank You" card signed by all the children. All present at the service were astonished and dumbfounded.

I was not looking forward to a heavenly union with Mrs Oshinowo, but that was what I had some months later. In a dream, I found myself in a big town, walking on a main road at the cool time of day. There, running towards me with open arms, was Mrs Oshinowo. She was brilliantly radiant, bubbling with life. She hugged and held me, full of thanks for all I had done for her while she was living. She told me that whilst in the hospital admission bed she had placed two requests before God. Firstly, for God to allow her to accomplish her life ambition by visiting Jerusalem before dying, and secondly to settle the rift between her eldest daughter and herself. She never discussed her requests with anybody ,but all the time she knew that my coming to her was the answer to her prayers. Action begins in Heaven when someone on Earth prays.

So my visit to the hospital was the answer to her prayers, and when I mentioned going on a pilgrimage, she knew there and then that God had granted her last wishes. God did it whilst she was depressed and had no strength. He raised her dead heart and dreams. God gave her hope and encouragement and she received it with faith.

Our heavenly Father knows what you need before you ask. There is power in silent prayer; we do not need to shout when in communion with God. He is not restricted by time, money or anything else. He is an unusual God doing unusual things. Our caring God knows everything and answers prayers.

Mrs Oshinowo told me that she had seen my mother. According to her, she lived in another area not too far from her. She said that she had congratulated my mother for giving birth to a child like me and leaving me behind on Earth to do marvellous things.

Mrs Oshinowo held my hands and prayed for me for a very long time. I felt as if her words were being injected into me. Her blessings on me were in abundance. She said it aloud to the hearing of all and sundry: "God will show the world that He is your God by how He will bless you". Her voice was still ringing in my ears as I woke up.

There are times in our lives when God puts us in situations where we cannot see, explain or understand. At such a time, all is for the glory of God to manifest, because all things work for God. He has a plan and purpose for everything created. We are not just wandering or meandering through life. He tested me on how to handle other people's problems, using me as the key to Mrs Oshinowo's lock. I felt more effective solving other people's problems than my own. Success depends on being a solution to others.

8. Burdens of Calling

My existence is a misery to me. It has never been easy from childhood – sickness, loneliness, hatred, divorce, bad relationship, rejection. But I have always felt the presence of God in every situation. I would have died but God stopped it. In my mind I know that God is definitely keeping me alive for His own purpose.

In 2000, I had a dream in which I was erecting a building. I engaged the services of many workers on site; builders, carpenters, plasterers, painters and many others. Some members of my extended family were also employed as operatives on the building site. My main duty was to travel around looking for and purchasing all the materials needed for the building construction. This was a tedious job for me. Sometimes, I would leave the site for over three months on purchasing assignments. On my return, I would bring all the necessary materials needed by all the operatives. Each of the workmen would take their needed materials. I was building with a team of takers!

I wore out my shoes and my patience walking up and down looking for building materials.

Whenever I showed up with materials, the operatives welcomed me with offensive remarks. They were abusive towards me, called me names and pushed me off the premises. My efforts meant nothing to them. They found my zeal irritating. None of them recognised me as the property owner. They were cruel and harsh towards me.

What really hurt most was their behaviour on site. Openly they urinated, defecated, threw personal rubbish around, splashed vomit on the walls. They behaved like wild animals; bullying and intimidating with no respect for themselves or others. It was emotionally and financially stressful to be around them. The construction of this building cost me insults, endurance and aggravations. It was a battle of heart and mind. I was pressed above measure and strength. I was burning off energy around the people who hated me. Their arrogance was devastating to my health. This pattern continued for quite a while. I suffered silently in their hands until I could not endure provocation no longer. They succeeded in draining the life out of me. I was depressed and discouraged.

As I could not take their condemnation any more, I decided to give up. This left us with an uncompleted building and unaccomplished mission. What a devastating consequence!

Stepping in with wit and inspiration, someone

arrived on the scene and greeted all the workmen on the construction site. His greetings totally drew their attention. His approach was authentically different; stunning, consistently luring. He spoke with authority.

Then I recognised Him. Christ my Lord and King; the Man with no limit. He was the one holding my hand. He spoke on my behalf. He spoke with a calm but commanding and irresistible tone. His voice was like roaring thunder, loud but soothing. Everybody and everything stood still on hearing His magical and extraordinary voice. He had stepped in just when it seemed all hope was lost.

Introducing Himself in the plurality of Authority, as the property owner, he asked all the workmen to draw closer to Him. He thanked them for their services in constructing the building. "Today, you will be paid your dues and wages," He told the workmen. "Whatever you wish for in life, be it a mansion, ship, jets, aeroplanes, fleet of cars, you will have. I will give you your hearts' desires, no matter how expensive they are.

"However, there is one clause. Out of the rubbish on this site, you need to make a replica of whatever you wish for. Make models out of the rubbish, use the faeces and urine as paints and decorations. Bring your models and I will approve them for you."

He sent them off to act on His instructions. Oops! the judgement of King Solomon, pulse-quickeningly good.

Immediately, they rushed back to the building site, scrabbling for all the rubbish they could find. Some openly argued and claimed ownership of faeces. On my right side, I recognised former church members running towards me. Speaking out of desperation and frustration, they claimed to have started defacing the building and now hearing that the Lord was rewarding only those presently working on the site, they rushed down for their own share of the booty. That left me shocked and confused, because never in life had I expected close associates in the vineyard to be the enemies within. However, God had made provision for my confusion.

A woman who was formerly a Lady Leader wept bitterly. She said "Mother, if only I had stayed with you. Your success reminds me of what I could have achieved in life". Let us allow God to take over situations in which we have no control. Their confessions surprised me so much because I never knew that whilst in the congregation, they were enemies in disguise.

After confession, the Lord gave them instruction to take off their clothes and dust all stains off the building. Positive confession brings salvation. With gladness, they yielded to His instruction. Walking stark naked, they climbed the loft, roof and everywhere to dust.

When the cleaning exercise finished, the glory of God was revealed. The building was dazzling; built on a magnificent scale with white marbles. I never knew that I was building a modern elegant Temple. God had called me to do something beyond my human ability.

Christ sent them off, carrying all the rubbish they had brought into the building. In His own words, Christ said, "They brought the rubbish into my House and now they have taken it away clinging on them". God took out of my life everything that should not be there.

Turning to me, as I was still standing beside him, Christ ushered me into the temple. The interior was radiant and spotless. I do not have words to describe the beauty and peace therein. The altar was the crowning glory with its extraordinarily elaborate decorations. It was huge and towered above anything around. The finishing was heavenly, awe inspiring; a phenomenon of achievement. It took me by surprise.

I was in the place of my transformation and identification. As I raised my voice up in praising the Living God, the Spirit inside of me woke up declaring the Glory of God.

9. Christ's Revelation - Pilgrimage Calling

In August 2001, our group of 22 Christian believers had completed all arrangements for the annual Holy Land pilgrimage. Air tickets, hotel confirmation and guide fees had been paid for far in advance. We were ready to go. Then there arose unexpectedly a disturbance between Israel and Palestine. The political and religious revolution was so severe that our Government placed an embargo on travelling to both countries. The government's decision was heart shattering. The tour organisers had spent so much on arrangements and were not willing to refund, and any hope of early settlement between the warring countries was sinking dangerously beneath the surface. So at our evening service on Friday, I had to announce to the congregation the cancellation of the pilgrimage.

Overnight, I had a dream. Sitting in front of my dressing table mirror, my daughter was busy brushing my hair and applying my make-up when suddenly the postman dropped a letter through the letter box. The sound of it dropping was so heavy, like a ton weight. Inquisitively I rushed downstairs to see the heavy object. Alas, it was just an envelope. But on picking it up and looking at it closely, I found that it was not an ordinary envelope. There was no stamp on it. Instead, the stamp space was perforated like the emergency wartime seal. The handwriting was of the old-time cursive style. More so, it was personally addressed to me in my native name! That aroused my curiosity. Nobody in the modern-day world knows my native name, the name given to me at birth by my parents. Modernity and Christianity had rubbed that off, replacing it with a baptismal English name. Who could the writer be who knew me by my long lost name?

Hurriedly opening it, I found that the letter was written on old foolscap ruled white sheet. Though handwritten, there was neither a scratch nor a stain of any sort. It was purity and perfection.

I sat down at my dressing table to read it. The four pages were full. The content was soul-searching, absorbing and heartfelt. The writer lamented my decision to cancel our Holy Land pilgrimage when all arrangements for a fitting welcome had been completed. I was accused of breaking my promise and thereby not being as good as my word. The letter went on to say that my betrayal was like that of a jilted bride at the altar. It was signed Emmanuel'.

I found the contents heartrending and shattering. The letter was utterly engrossing and exceptionally moving. No wonder my eyes were full of wailing and dripping tears.

Without saying a word, I rushed out and headed straight to my local church to see Elder Emmanuel, who was one of the Ministers, thinking that he had sent the letter. I was determined to have a brawl and intended to shout and cry my denial of all the accusations he had written to me. Fortunately Elder Emmanuel was at the Church. He was so surprised to see me in such a disturbed state. Vehemently denying all accusations, he looked stunned and dazed. Gently he told me that he was not the writer but was sure the letter had been written the by greatest Emmanuel – Jesus Christ!

Returning home in a flash and flying up the stairs, I looked for the letter, but it was gone. What could have happened? How come the letter had disappeared? My daughter, the hairdresser, explained that she had seen me reading the letter but had not seen any writing on the paper. To her, the foolscap ruled white sheet appeared blank. She was surprised that I could read from a blank sheet.

Retracing my steps back to the stairway to see if I had dropped it in a hurry, I flew down the stairs. Suddenly I found myself on a major street in Jerusalem and walking towards me was Christ, my Saviour. He was beaming with smiles whilst holding out His hands towards me for an embrace. Gladly He drew me into His arms. He confirmed writing and sending me the letter to show his disappointment for our cancellation. I explained the facts surrounding my decision, my visit to Elder Emmanuel and all the efforts I had made to find the letter. Laughing with amusement, Christ told me that He was aware of my flight and my plight. He was watching me running amok. Jokingly, he said assumption makes an ass out of you.

Back to the facts of life. Christ told me that He had brought me over in spirit to Jerusalem because there were some hidden truths he wanted to share with me. We entered the old Jerusalem City through St Stephen's Gate. Leading me through Jerusalem's main market, He was walking at a run and I could not keep up with him. He urged me to walk briskly, as most of the traders were Muslims and would kill anyone who dared confess to be a Christian. Lifting up a Muslim praying mat, and revealing a hole dug underneath, Christ told me that the hole contained the blood of Christian believers killed for the sake of allegiance to Christ. He said that there would come a time of great massacre in Jerusalem when Christians would suffer at the hands of persecutors, a time when Muslims in Jerusalem would have zero tolerance for other faiths. Many followers would deny their faith, but Champions would fight and stand up even unto death. There is a difference between Champions and followers.

He told me that a time of transition was coming and Believers should not expect to be liked. Rather we should prepare our victuals; prepare for what to do next when what we expected did not work.

My response to his advice was in the negative. I told Him that with all I had seen in Israel, nobody would take my belief away from me. Touching my forehead as if to drive the point home, Christ reminded me that whenever the enemy attacks, he comes against what we know about God.

Christ and I had very deep conversations which I will not disclose in this book. They are reserved and sealed.

Ascending to Mount Zion through the low valley via the Church of All Nations way, Christ took me to the point where He wept over Jerusalem. We walked round the garden and finally stood looking towards the Old City. Christ told me that not long from now, all places indicating his life in Israel, presently preserved for history, would be taken down and destroyed. So anyone who has the opportunity to visit Israel should not waste time.

Christ showed up to show me who I am. He called me out to be a Captain, leading his people to Him. Prior to this revelation, I thought I was helping and enabling friends to fulfil their dreams. Never did it occur to me that pilgrimage empowerment is part of my calling. This pilgrimage task defines who I am.

My journey back was by the same route. He led me back to our meeting point and bade me goodbye for now.

I woke up instantly. Without wasting any more time, I picked up the phone, calling all intended pilgrims to get ready. Only two people refused to travel. We had a wonderful pilgrimage.

One of the two people who did not perform the pilgrimage with us in 2001 had another opportunity 14 years later. He joined my pilgrimage group in 2015 and at the Brook of Elisha in Jericho, Pastor Brown, out of his own free will, came out to narrate this story. He did regret not following the spiritual instruction as revealed by Christ and it took him 14 years to accomplish his pilgrimage dream. He is now a regular pilgrim to Israel as a pilgrimage leader.

I am significant because there is something inside of me that Christ is using. He called out of me who I am.

10. Christ's Revelation: Transformed by a Vision

Success is hard-won when you are leading a small church, but all the sweeter for it. All obstacles in my way have nothing to do with me. The fight is always over what is in me. They are against God's mission on my life, but by the grace of God my persistence, passion and patience will pay off.

In 2003, the local church, Holy Trinity Family Chapel (UK), where I hold the Ministerial post, was under pressure, with the painful uncertainty of securing accommodation for community uses. Then I had this dream. I met a long-time friend who had just returned from a journey. We exchanged greetings and he apologised profusely for not replying to my letters on time. My response was not far-fetched, as I did not receive any response from him. Apologetically, he volunteered to take me round the city in order to show me the contents of his long-lost written reply. He took me to a very popular spiritual church in a neighbouring borough. He stood outside while He asked me to go inside, telling me that whatever I saw in the church was what He had written in his response to me.

As I entered the church, I saw the Minister. He

welcomed me, ushering me towards a corner chair. Lying in front of the altar were many old and new money bags. I asked him who they belonged to and why they were displayed openly. His response was shocking. The money bags represented his church members, both old and new, and the contents were the fortunes and assets belonging to them. He said that he had access to them anytime without being queried. Bending down to pick up some of the money bags, he called out the names of the owners and how long each had been worshipping under him. I stood there perplexed.

Just then, he asked to be excused. He took his time returning. Then I saw his spouse speeding out. Despite my loud greetings, she did not glance at me, so I ran after her just to exchange greetings properly. I reached for her dress to draw her attention. Turning round, I saw what she was carrying in her hands. A bowl of human waste! "Oh! That's my role; that's what I do every day, that's why he kept me under his belt and spell," she concluded.

For a moment, the world stood still. Spinning and rotating back to life, I took to my heels. When I got to my waiting friend, he did not look surprised to see me crying. He sat me down to tell me some bitter home truths. Analysing the facts, he said: "There is the little truth and the larger truth. I always tell the larger one. Sometimes it is not easy to separate things. There are stages we must go through before God can manifest

His promises in our life. He has to take us through the process before getting to the promises. Circumstances have nothing against God's words." He stared at me long enough for me to recognise who He was, Christ my Lord and Saviour. I trembled before him.

He asked me if I understood the scenes in the church, and my answer was in the affirmative. He said He had taken me to places where He did not take anybody else. He said that regrettably, some church ministers were stingy and stinking filthy. They were not people of righteous character. They were worshipping the devil and its monetary agents but with little endurance, God will give us the wealth of the wicked and the unjust as inheritance.

Continuing His words of advice, Christ added: "If you cannot do what your mates are doing, then you have no option but to wait for God's time. Stop grumbling. Appreciate your calling, because it is the promise which you have got. Believe in your dream, even when other people are mocking you. It is yours, not theirs. Hard times come before the biggest breakthrough. Be strong and courageous. Fight your inner insecurity, fear and doubt. Rely on your inner strength to endure and win. The gain is in the pain. You are almost there."

He tapped my shoulder to continue our visit to another church. I declined with a passionate promising plea that I had seen enough and would never grumble again. Christ escorted me back home and bade me goodbye. I woke up wandering on which planet I was. Alas! I was still on Planet Earth.

11. A Near Death Experience

When sickness struck in 2010, nobody thought I would survive because I was on the verge of giving up the ghost due to undiagnosed illness. Daily visits to my GP became a routine. The doctor who saw me at the medical centre referred me to the general hospital as she did not know what else to do. On arrival at her clinic, she called me aside and said "I could see that you are seriously sick but I do not know what is wrong with you. I do not want to lose you, so I am making an urgent referral to the general hospital."

What started off as an ordinary chest irritation gradually developed, but the diagnosis by the senior clinicians at the university teaching hospital was inconclusive. Many medical tests, including X-rays, blood and other specimens were carried out, but nothing conclusive came of them. Within a period of eight weeks, I lost half of my body weight, looking frail and dehydrated. Panic arose in the family as they watched me just fading slowly away and nobody had a clue what was wrong or what to do.

All praise to God, because though I was losing almost everything, my mind was sound. My mind was my power. My head was clear, so I could think. I sent for those who are close to me. My cousin, Mrs Lawuyi, her husband, and my mentor Dr Michael Fajoye. They were awed at the situation. My dear husband was doting on me with care and affection. So also were my daughters Abi and Rachel. It was not fair on them, it was not right, but I was in a transition and I could not help it.

Then I had a dream. I packed for a journey, but had to lodge at a guest house while we were being prepared for the journey ahead. I was kept in a small room; very weary, lonely and sad I was. At the end of the three days' transition, we were air freighted in a giant balloon, which landed in an out-of-world airport the size of an earthly state. At this airport an uncountable number of balloons and planes were landing every minute, conveying human cargos from all over the world and other known and unknown places. The entry border was a long building with watchtowers. Every area was censored.

On entering the building, there was orderliness in vetting. Despite the fact that there were numerous passengers trying to check in, all was calm; no pushing, no grumbling, no hassling. Another thing which I observed was that none of us carried luggage or passports. All we had was the clothes on us.

There were several thousand manned check-in counters. When it was my turn, I approached one for entry clearance. Overhead, staring at me was a gentleman. He drew closer to me for inspection and interrogation. That was strange, because all my fellow passengers had passed through the border without being questioned.

He turned me around to peel a small label stuck on my back. He stared at it for a long time before opening his mouth to question me.

"Where are you coming from?" he asked.

"From the earth," I replied.

"Who did all these to you?" was his second question.

"All what?" I questioned.

"All these" he replied waving the fingers of his right hand at the label held in his left hand.

"I do not know what you mean," I said. Then he explained to me.

"Where you are coming from, you have been back slashed, stabbed, raped, cheated, and hacked. For God's sake, who are these people?" he queried.

"I do not know them," I responded.

He began his analysis, reading from the label and stating the dates, times, and places where atrocities had been committed against my soul. He named the culprits responsible. My response was to thank him for his care and pity towards me but I asked him to just allow me in, to pass me across the border, because I was so tired and just wanted to go home and rest.

He bluntly refused me entry. Looking down at me with swelling tears in his eyes, he said "You will never rest if you cross over now, because your soul will be crying for vengeance against those who committed these evil deeds against you. You really do not know what they did to you. They are wicked and your soul will never forget. So I am sending you back to earth to go and iron it out with them. Forgiveness is the gift you give yourself. Go back and forgive them; and come back after. Only then will your soul rest in peace."

It was then I recognised Him, Christ my Lord and Master once again. He was the compassionate Manager. "Yes, it is Me," He whispered into my ears. "I am the First Born, the Dead and Risen Christ. Go back, for it is not yet your time".

He beckoned to a floor supervisor and instructed him to stop the plane from taking off as I had to return immediately. Arguing, I told him that I was already dead, but he said to me "You did not die, although you looked like you did. You will live and flow again".

Events after that were like magic. From nowhere, two electric skating boards were fixed on to my feet, carrying me back to the airfield. The skates were controlled by in-built spirit. They never collided with anyone or anything, even though the airport was full of people. They never missed their destination. I was taken to the right plane, which took off immediately on command, returning me to earth.

The sickness dragged on for over six months. By this time, the doctor had placed me on three different daily medications and was monitoring every change. I had memory nightmares of my childhood sickness and fears. My ghosts of the past and anxiety about the future overwhelmed me. The pressure on me was too much.

Then one snowy night, I had an out of body experience. Slipping out of my room, I followed a shining light which directed me to a house on the outskirts of the city. There was an upper waiting room which was of moderate size, full of people of all ages, females and males alike. We were all on our feet, on alert in readiness for a voyage. Randomly, the shining light would lead more people to the room and would leave again in search of more. This was the pattern for days. On one of its rounds, it brought back a small child, a six-year-old boy. He looked so handsome and innocent. He did not know where he was; he looked lost in transit. His innocent look aroused my pity, and I went over to comfort him. This child told me that he was sick with intestinal worms, but his mother did not know what was wrong. He would not have died had he been dewormed. Such a little oversight caused his death!

By this time, the shining light had gone on another soul-hunting round. The waiting and the anxiety were too much and it was unbearable for me. In an irrational moment I stormed out of the room in a rage to stand on the balcony, telling the room occupants to call me whenever they were ready to move on. I just wanted to be on my own for some seconds.

Just then, the very moment I stepped out, there

was a strong breeze. It brushed pass me and took all the people in the room away with it in a flash. The room was empty. I rushed back into the room to see if anyone was left behind, but there was not a soul. Everyone was taken. It was as if there was a rapture. I felt lost for words, confused and dazed. Standing on the balcony, I was thinking within me, replaying the record of events which had taken place in the room, but talking aloud to myself in circles and riddles. I found myself in a solitary confinement; very lonely.

Whilst standing on the balcony, I saw two old women walking down the road towards the house. They were both well over 90 years old; both had walking sticks, and it took them a long time to cover a short distance, stopping to rest after taking a few steps. They were walking like millipedes.

The elder of the two spoke to me from a distance. She asked me if the entourage had gone. My answer was positive. "Yes, they have just gone, leaving me behind. I just came on to the balcony for fresh air and just at that moment a strong breeze emptied the room in a matter of seconds."

"Ah! You are the lucky one. Your time is not yet up. You have a second chance in a worse place. Just because you were brought here does not mean that your timing was right," the old woman said. Looking over her shoulder, pointing to her companion, she continued to enlighten me. "We are both old and our time is up, and that is why we come here willingly.

Nobody came to raid us from our homes. We did not know each other while on earth but we met on our homeward journey," she said.

The second elderly woman said, "Every morning, the Creator gives His permission for the Spirit of Death to go out and raid living beings, be it men, beasts, flying birds, creeping things and fish. Any living thing that receives the mark will not last that day. All souls are gathered and escorted on a daily basis". Standing under the balcony slab, she said to me, "When you belong to God, God will have His way. Go back home. This sickness will not kill you". There and then I had a feeling that I would survive.

12. A supernatural realm journey

A supernatural realm journey is rare but when it occurs, it is cherished by true worshippers of the Most High. There God reveals to believers only, not to the entire world, because ordinary people cannot understand things being kept in secret places. However, believers like me see, hear and dream because God shows all. All these are possible because of constant spiritual worship and interactions.

A very close friend of mine, Enoh, died in 2007 at the age of 60 years. She was the kindest and most humble human being I had ever known, a doting mother to her children and a dutiful wife to her husband. She had a good and deeply fulfilled life but unfortunately death snatched her away in her middle years. Her death left a vacuum in my life because she was a great confidant.

Some months after her death, my guarding spirit took me on a journey to the spiritual world. There waiting for me was my friend. Was she happy to see me? Yes, she was. She said that after her death, she had visited me many times to console me, but because I was deep in grief I did not notice her presence. Without wasting any time, she invited me to her residence. We stood outside a thatched, windowless old house whilst she explained her circumstances to me. Apparently since her death she had been standing outside this house because two occupants living in refused to leave, claiming that she owed them maintenance fees. That excuse aroused my anger. So without thinking twice, I marched to the house and faced the illegal occupants. They were a couple, very polite and soft spoken.

Their explanations baffled me. They said that when my friend had left on the journey 60 years ago, she had promised to be sending them maintenance fees, but nothing was received. Bringing out a ragged bag, they claimed that my friend's bank account was empty because no deposit had been remitted. For them to vacate the house, they needed to be paid maintenance fees as their dues. My friend agreed with them, blaming her husband for not allowing her to give alms and donations to the needy. She said that while she was the only one providing for the family, her earthly husband was stingy and a money monger.

I was not pleased with her excuses. So I reminded her of church tithes, Easter retreat donations and regular alms to the poor as preached and practised. In defence she blamed her husband for denying her the chance to fulfil her acts of charity. So, once more, she was locked outside her home.

Just then a thought came to my mind. I reminded Enoh that both our parents were dead and if only we could find them maybe my friend could stay with them temporarily. She said that she knew where our departed parents were, but she was too shy to visit them. Enoh explained that our parents now had some children living with them. That surprised me a lot because they were very old. No, not that they delivered new babies, far from that. Our departed parents were now looking after the children we had aborted on earth. Apparently the abortions committed were recorded against our names and when our parents died, they were united with the waiting souls of their grandchildren.

Enoh could not visit them as she had no gifts for the departed souls. She was ashamed of her guilt. I volunteered to visit and speak on her behalf, but she refused. My friend now explained to me that she had invited me to see her ordeal so that I would not fall into the same when my time comes. She made me promise to be kind and generous to everyone, even if they took my generosity to be stupidity. One of the ways of knowing that you are good is when people take you for granted. The people you take places are the ones that disappoint you.

13. Visiting Living Stream City

God is the ultimate and absolute power. The key to the secret places is with the Most High and only to those chosen are the revelations made known. The spiritual gift He gave me has taken me to places where my characters won't keep me.

I was given the grace of spiritual journey to the Living Stream City. The City is peaceful and all buildings were bungalows; there were no high rise buildings. Each building was framed in between four surrounding walls of beautiful, flourishing flowers. Something peculiar about the gardens was that on touching a petal, the flowers would start singing melodious tunes. They were recreational flowers.

The city roads were of glass, polished and shiny. There were no vehicles or planes. Moreover, there was no need for road sweepers because there was a stream running through the city which cleaned and cleared away all debris. It was the city of the living, running stream.

While walking around, I could feel the gentle pushing current of the stream. At first, the level was to my ankles, but gradually it rose to the hem of my garment and upwards to my knees. By now, the current was stronger and more forceful, so I decided to seek refuge in a nearby building until the water slowed down.

The Spirit within me directed my feet to a house. It now occurred to me that although the stream flowed all around the city, it never entered the houses; it stopped at the threshold. What a sensitive living stream. This great stream moved by instinct.

On opening the front door, I entered a church, and the whole building was filled with the beautiful, soothing voices of a choir. To my surprise, the front usher, dressed in white ceremonial military uniform, welcomed me with salutations before announcing my entry as Captain Mother. The usher then marched down to the basement, where people of higher rank had convened. On his return, he showed me a beautiful throne, and gestured to me to sit with them.

Theirs was a beautiful and spectacular worship service which I found intimate and profoundly moving. God's presence was there. I could sense and see it in the worship, giving tangible offerings to God in praise. Their worship was a sacrifice of praise in spiritual hymns. Their hymnal rhythm brought me spiritually flowing before the Lord.

Eventually, I knelt down in humble adoration to pray. Whilst still praying, I was overwhelmed with calmness running through me; I felt peace in my soul and healed in my spirit.

Bidding them farewell, I left to return home, to my base.

Chapter 17

JERUSALEM - ISRAEL PILGRIMAGES

Jerusalem is a glorious, majestic city, the most famous city on earth. The combination of ability and creativity has brought about modern changes in the city. Jerusalem lies between two mountains – Moriah and Zion. Great, beautiful and remarkable buildings cling to the slopes with their strong, defensive walls surrounding the old city. Everywhere you look, there is a reflection of wealth and determination. What a unique place to be. I was told that some peoples' daily pledge is to live, defend and even die for this great celestial city. Is it worth dying for? Yes, it is. You need to see it in its glory. It is the earthly city of our heavenly Father and God.

Jerusalem, to me, is a place where God resides; a place of extreme devotion and the source of holiness. A mystical and universal city. It is heaven on earth full of divine providence.

Jerusalem is a religious centre and the shrine of three major faiths – Judaism, Christianity and Islam. From the few facts in my knowledge, I find it to be a beautiful city. Its previous earthly rulers were powerful, ambitious and wise. King Solomon was one; so was his father King David before him. Jerusalem is a city of devotion. Everywhere you look, you see the crucifixion image.

I have had the privilege of leading both practising Christians and ambitious new converts to Christianity on annual group pilgrimages to Israel since 1995. This has opened my mind to the intensity of religion. I was captivated by Jerusalem's spiritual aura. The Grace of God in my life put me in this position. It is beyond my understanding, ability and knowledge. God promoted me in His Grace to lead His people back to Him. What a privilege! Whenever I visit Israel, I feel as if God is bringing me before Kings. I treasure every moment in the Holy Land, the spiritual gifts I receive but most importantly the Giver of my Life and gifts – GOD.

The planning, tour and accomplishment are a joy

and an irresistible delight from start to finish. Most of our tour guides are good, but the best guide is an Israeli Rabbi, Amnon Betseer. His moving, absorbing and wonderful illustrations are fabulous teachings. Amnon is wise and poignant. He is a brilliant teacher.

Holy Trinity family pilgrimage talks, lectures and services bring the Holy Bible to life. Our pilgrimages are masterful and expert arrangements provided for the comfort of all pilgrims. For the past twenty-two years, we have ensured that all pilgrimage participants have a taste of the heavenly delights which Israel and Jerusalem in particular, have to offer. We all feel spiritually and perfectly pampered in Israel. Sincerely speaking, I am addicted to these successful pilgrimages.

People perform Israel holy land pilgrimages for many intimate reasons. Some go to Israel for healing, to be free of sadness, debt, sickness, lamentation, or for victory, blessings, spiritual development, getting closer to God, and so forth. However, unknown to many, some pilgrims go to the Holy Land to surrender to God and die because they are tired of running, tired of life's hurdles. Their belief is that Israel is the gateway to heaven and therefore it is a privilege to die there. I have had instances of pilgrims who intentionally travelled with me knowing full well that they were on their last legs. They wanted to go over to the other side assuring themselves that Christ was in the boat with them. I do not blame them. God is the

Performing a baptism in the River Jordan

greatest Judge, as He holds all the answers. God has been very good to me and my pilgrimage groups for over twenty years, with no fatal incidents.

Pilgrimage leadership is a great task and God has given me what it takes to bear the burden and reap the benefits. It has not always been smooth sailing as there have been many stumblings, but as an established church we have been able to withstand blows which a new church might not survive.

Stumbling sometimes happens for correction. On a pilgrimage in 2010, my group was placed in a guesthouse which offered less than we had paid for. We had paid for 4-star hotel accommodation in Jerusalem. At dinner, we were lined up like

Holy Land (Israel) Pilgrims, led by Captain Mother Hasson

schoolchildren holding our plates for meal portions. It was a sorry sight. I challenged the guesthouse owner, a 90-year-old Arab man, and he just brushed me off. I stood my ground and told him that we would be checking out of his guest house the next day. Without having supper, I went straight to my room. Not long after, when I was not quite asleep, the door opened slightly and a pipe-smoker was puffing tobacco fumes into my bedroom. It was the guesthouse owner. His aim was to induce me into a deep slumber before inflicting punishment for challenging and standing up to him in defence of my group.

I jumped up shouting and repeatedly calling on the name of "God of Abraham". The intruder left, saying he did not know that I believed in the God of Abraham. "I thought you worshipped idols," he said. "So you worship the living God. I am sorry". You must always be on the lookout for the anti-Christ elements and force them to retreat.

The following morning as I was leaving my bedroom, I found a bouquet of flowers by my door. On entering the dining room, the guesthouse owner walked towards me to offer an embrace. Begging me for forgiveness, he apologised for his malicious visit to my room. He said his intrusion had been the act of a deluded, foolish old man. As a leader, you do not know what you have got until you are chased to a stumbling ground.

At breakfast, the tables were laid as if for royalty. We were served with the best cutlery and china dishes full of mouth-watering food, but my group members refused to eat because of the previous night's episode at dinner. I had to retract my instructions and plead for tolerance. To prove maturity, you must adjust your expectations in the middle of a crisis so as to survive. A little thing out of place may cause great pain.

God allows things to happen for reasons best known to Him. We are here to serve and help others increase their joy and attain their potential. We are problem solvers, as our contributions make a difference. However, at times there is a price to pay.

On the 7th August 2016, on the Mount of Transfiguration in Israel, leading my pilgrimage group to a shed for solitary prayers, an incident occurred that no one had expected. It was a hot sunny day. As there were two elderly pilgrims amongst us, I stayed behind with them chatting and encouraging them because the heat was unbearable. The group was already sitting and waiting for me to start ministerial administration. As we stepped in, one of the elderly women with me just asked "Mother, what is a snake doing in our tent?" That baffled me, as I saw no snake. She insisted, pointing at the direction of the altar where I was supposed to stand to deliver the lecture. Then all of a sudden we all saw the curled serpent. We all ran out in panic. If I had left the elderly women behind, I would have been bitten by the snake as it lay in wait for me. As I always say, an act of kindness never kills anyone.

During the August 2017 holy pilgrimage, my group was holding an open-air sermon service when from nowhere a bee flew into our midst and found its way into my gown, stinging me. The attack was so severe that I almost pulled my clothes off on the spot. Fortunately for me, my group members rushed to unbutton my gown and help crush it, but not before it had stung me all over my back, arm and neck. I was almost paralysed on one side of my body.

To my fellow spiritualists reading this book, from my personal experience, the fact that you are valued is the reason you are being attacked. Hold on to your faith in God, as you will never lose His integrity. You are what God created you to be. When the storm is over, you will rise, just like me.

Prophetess Eunice Aisha Okeke (JP) carrying her cross in Jerusalem during Stations of the Cross congregational prayers, in unison to God

Chapter 18

MY MOMENT OF RELIGIOUS JOY – CAPTAIN MOTHER ORDINATION

To every Spiritualist reading this book, please adhere to words of wisdom. Remember to prophesy positively into your own life. What you say about yourself becomes life. Pray for yourself and hear yourself saying it. Whatever you ask of God in prayers shall be granted unto you. Your tongue is the sword of the mouth. Use your tongue for self-defence, victory and blessings. Speak to yourself in prayers as I do every day. By so doing, you spiritually build up your inner self, so that whatever happens outside, you have the inner spirit to support you. As a spiritualist, you are strengthened by the inner spirit. You have to know who you are before anybody else knows who you are. Whatever you feel in the physical starts in the spiritual realm.

Please do not doubt your spiritual calling. You may not see it now, but it will manifest. Do not collapse. Press on, walk on, go by what you hear. God will bring us to our destiny by hearing. Do not look at your deformity or any shortcomings.

There is nothing as powerful as the Spirit of Endurance; it is the secret of life.

I live and function in Christ. I do not just walk with Him. I do not walk alongside Him. There is a great difference between being in Christ, living and functioning in Christ and walking with Christ. He carries me wherever He goes; always in communion and fellowship with Christ. I am sure of whom I am in Christ because He handpicked me. It is a wonderful feeling to be chosen. I can see now why I had to go through storms in life. I went beyond my reflection, beyond my background and education. I went above myself because God is in control. Trust yourself to do big things in God.

So, my Lord and my God prepared a spectacular consecration service for Himself on Sunday 3rd

September 2017 and robed me in as a Bride. What an amazing sight! To me, it was a wedding feast and Christ was the Groom. With God, the honeymoon never ends.

I was solemnly enthroned as a Captain Mother by twelve anointed Church Leaders and Elders, each holding in his or her hands the Holy Bible representing the fruit of defined Revelations, a bottle of Holy Land olive oil, bottle of Holy Land Zion wine and Ministerial Stoles from Israel. That was my greatest day, an exciting celebration of a new age.

The signature that approved my ordination as a Captain Mother was from God. It is who you know that enables you to prosper in life, not what you know. I know my God whom I serve, and He knows me.

It was an iconic event in that the presiding senior Leader at this eventful occasion was Father Olu Abiola, OBE. His father, the late Baba Aladura Abiola, ordained me in 1975 as an Aladura (the lowest rank) in Ile-Ife, Nigeria. This was an example of the old bringing life to the new. Who could have foretold that forty-two years later his son would ordain me as a Captain Mother, the highest women's rank in the established Order.

At my ordination service as Captain Mother, I got my joy and glory back. My status rose with my new name. Hallelujah! It was a tremendously important event of my life; more than anyone could imagine. I felt drenched in success. Success is when what you see inside materialises outside. I thank God for my integrity, which is very rare. There is no precedent for what God is doing in my life. Mine is the first and He is doing it in style. God got me ready to step into the next dimension.

I was filled with the feelings of a winner and enjoyed every moment of it. I totally forgot the past cheating, hatred and victimisation and I am now enjoying where I am and what I have, a boost of love and encouragement. I am moving on in the agenda of Christ who calls and fills me up to function. Whatever the Lord puts in my spirit, I just do it. It is already inside me. I do not wait for the approval of man. I walk with confidence before God. God placed in my spirit a greater vision which was higher than my imagination. He has given me something more important than how I feel. The Hand of God was on me. I could hear His voice telling me what to do, but I felt so little and unworthy of the Grace He was bestowing of me.

Also, I was afraid of breaking the established rules of the Church whereby ordination has to be through authoritative ranks. If you do not follow the earthly system, those in power will cast you out and lock you out. What do you do if you do not compare with the person you are being compared with?

We often forget that God does great things in strange places.

Authority is a master of systems and in strict implementation, there is no room for your faith. Let us put away the system that is killing us. The system does not give anything to anyone until that person is successful. We live in an age of religious extremism when people wait for private personalised glory.

I really agree with and support the idea that we must have orderliness in the House of God, but so also must we be free of religious obsession. There is a big difference between religion and relationship. We must not be religious to the point of missing the Revelations.

At last, I followed the rhythm and pace of the inner spirit within me. I stopped worrying and being anxious. I had to confront the conflicts within me before confronting the conflicts around me. I believe that what God has given me is enough to defeat my fear.

God has been shaping me to fit into this position. It is a spiritual set up, and this is the season of coming into my uniqueness. The Most High was about to put me in a position that felt too big for me. God was immersing me beyond myself. I was not ready to submit to objections. After all, it is my own vision, message and mission. I have been through too much to be intimidated, even if I have to go differently. My potential is in the Lord Jesus and my life is already predetermined.

Those who objected did not hear what I was hearing; they are spiritually dead.

I was focusing on my Lord's directives, as I now realised that my present circumstances were a set up for His plan. Not much was done by me in preparation, as the Lord had prepared everything years in advance without me knowing. I did not enlist the help of anyone with my preparations. God had put all my attire and ornaments in certain places many years before my big day. My vestment was made of crown and pomegranate cloth of gold, a turn of the century design. It is an extraordinary costume, and it made a statement with its glamorous gold trimmings. It was extravagantly gorgeous. The biggest joy is the one you get unexpectedly.

As a Church Minister, I usually dress functionally but stylishly. However, now that the Lord, Christ, the Name Changer has called me by a new name, I must dress functionally but presentably, because graceful posture is the key to attraction and attention. Personality is a gift, and not everybody has it.

I am a bit of a perfectionist. I look at something and settle only for the best. I strive to maintain high standards. I am unique and exceptional.

Everything that happened to me in my life prepared me for my present role and the purpose for which God had predestined me. What went 'wrong' was right for what God wanted to do in my life. In fact, my 'disasters' were actually directions.

I carry the anointing in the presence of God. The good Lord gave me the hard times so that I could

Enthronement and Ordination Service as a Captain Mother

Receiving Congregational and Authoritative Blessings

appreciate the good ones. I came from nothing, so I appreciate everything. Life is not always fair, but God is always faithful.

I will continue to enjoy my current position, fully remembering all the goodness He had done for me. Godliness with contentment is a great gain.

I have been planted by God, not buried. With all the odds, God says to me "Live" and here I am still living and not just existing. God concealed my destiny by planting it deep in the soil, but He reveals Himself in my life now at the season of my harvesting. My work in the Vineyard is part of the legacy I am leaving for my children, grandchildren and even people yet unborn.

Height of Glory

As for the future, whatever in front of me is more important than what is behind me. With the guidance of God, I will always find my way and everything will line up with my destiny and new name - Captain Mother serving people, even if they are not appreciative. God has made me an institutional blessing to my community.

I have learnt that I may not reap where I sow, but God will make it up to me. There is more in me than can be seen. God's favour makes me effective and my Ministry, Holy Trinity Family Chapel (UK) and all the parishioners will be favoured as well in God's defined purpose. God is going to do good things in our lives. I am looking ahead to what God has in store for me so that I can see how my purpose fits into His plan. The best is yet to come.

My latter days shall be greater than my early days, as God's blessings will make up for all the foolish mistakes and failures in my life. I will be celebrated and nobody will rob me of my celebrations.

My cheerfulness and brightness in my old age are joys that come from my soul.

With God's magnificent blessings, I have a crown of success and happiness. I am healed, saved and blessed. As Christ is the Prize, I will endure to the end of the race. I am connected to Him, so therefore I am a Winner. Life is not about starting well, but about finishing well. Thanks to God who is in control of My Being and Calling.

www.ingramcontent.com/pod-product-compliance
Lightning Source LLC
Chambersburg PA
CBHW061943070426
42450CB00007BA/1031